Stop Negative Self-Talk

How to Rewire Your Brain to Think Positively

By: Dana Williams

Edited by Dawn Wooten

Table of Contents

Preface 5

Part I: Brain Games 7

    Chapter 1: What Is Self-Talk? 9

    Chapter 2: How the Brain Generates Self-Talk........... 13

    Chapter 3: How to Recognize the Negative Voice 16

Part II: Identify and Confront 34

    Chapter 4: Defining the Positive and Negative Self-Talk 39

    Chapter 5: What Leads Us to Negative Self-Talk 44

Part III: Treatment and Recovery Strategies 55

    Chapter 6: Options for Treatment 59

Part IV: Looking Within 83

    Chapter 7: The Energy of the Mind............................ 84

    Chapter 8: Them's Freudin' Words.............................. 87

    Chapter 9: Find Your Powerful Voice.......................... 91

Part V: Rewire Your Brain 98

    Chapter 10: Be Self-Empowered 99

    Chapter 11: Quiet the Negative Voice......................... 106

    Chapter 12: Consciously Rewire Your Brain 109

    Chapter 13: The Process 113

    Chapter 14: Categorize Your Memories 156

    Chapter 15: Take Back the Power 165

    Chapter 16: Find Your Positive Energy 168

Chapter 17: Eliminate Your Negative Energy............ 172

Chapter 18: Tap into Your Strength—Mental and Spiritual ... 180

Chapter 19: Visualize Your Future without NST 184

Afterword... 189

References... 191

Preface

Darcy was always told to stop being so negative. She was always asked what was wrong or why she was depressed. Darcy isolated herself from others to avoid contaminating them with the roiling imp inside her mind. She was afraid to tell anyone about what she was hearing in the quiet spaces of her mind: "Why do you even bother?" "You think he's cute? Yeah, right, he wouldn't look twice at you." "Just stay in—you know no one cares what you think anyway."

What Darcy didn't know was that her own mind was working against her.

It's that little voice inside your head - some people call it the devil on their shoulders. People identify you as a cynic. Maybe you've been called a pessimist or misanthrope. However you have labeled yourself or your mind, this phenomenon is known as *Negative Self-Talk* (NST). It's when the thoughts in our heads are despondent, depressive, or defeated. The thoughts make us appear bitter, bleak, or barren. The gloomy Gus in the room is always the one who enters feeling hopeful but allows NST to drive them out feeling hopeless.

Once you start down the road of listening to negative self-talk, it is a road that is difficult to get off. Performing a successful U-turn on the road of negative self-talk takes a great deal of effort, knowledge, discipline, and courage. It's a scary thing to be saddled with NST and not know how to get out of it. There is a lot we have to learn before we can start working on getting rid of it.

How do our brains create negative self-talk? What fuels that negative energy with perpetual motion? What do mental health experts say about negative self-talk? How can we manage it? Can we really rewire our brains to expel the naysayer and its endless supply of non-affirming rhetoric?

The answers are here! In *Stop Negative Self-Talk: How to Rewire Your Brain to Think Positively*, we will explore the inner workings of the mind, read stories of people with familiar problems of NST, examine ways to recognize and eliminate negative self-talk, and educate ourselves on this single truth:

I HAVE THE POWER TO THINK FOR MYSELF!

Part I: Brain Games

All of our thoughts start in the brain. Our brains are made up of billions of neurons (a type of cell) that communicate with one another via electrical impulses (neurotransmitters). When these neurons start firing back and forth, a thought forms. The foundation for the thought comes from information gathered through the senses—what we see, hear, smell, taste, and touch—as well as our memories, which provide details and data to help our neurons formulate thoughts (Chodosh, 2016).

We have millions of thoughts every day. Some we are aware of, and some we are not. Let's say you want to pick up the remote and turn on the television. In order to do that, you first have the thought, "I want to watch television." Then we think, "Where is the remote?" Next we think, "Aha! There it is!" when we find it. We then have a series of thoughts responsible for picking up the remote, looking at the buttons, locating the on button, pressing the on button, and looking at the television to see if it has turned on. Those are the thoughts we are aware of.

What we aren't aware of are the instructions our brain is passing out to different parts of the body: instructions to the eyes to find the remote, instructions to the hand to pick up the remote, instructions to the eyes to find the right button, instructions to the finger to press the button, and instructions to the eyes to look up at the television. These involuntary thoughts are certainly present, but we don't need to keep track of them in our conscious mind. What if we could, though?

If we were able to consciously access both the known and unknown thoughts in our brains, we might have a better chance of controlling our self-talk. Scientists in biology and psychology are continuously studying how the brain works, and their findings may lead us to a useful, proactive understanding of the brain and how we might be able to access it consciously. If we could do that, maybe we could stop NST altogether. Wouldn't that be something?

Chapter 1: What Is Self-Talk?

It is not unusual for a person to hear "that little voice inside" telling them things. This can vary from a positive affirmation—"Way to go on that project!"—to a devastating slap of negativity-- "Seriously, that's the best you can do?" Oftentimes, people will relate those voices to harsh voices from the past, such as overly critical relatives or authority figures—parents, grandparents, teachers, pastors, coaches, mentors, friends, and even bullies are some examples—all of whom may have no way of knowing that their negativity and harsh criticisms could cause long-term damage.

When you grow up with this type of negativity in your environment, it is not unusual to experience negative self-talk throughout your life. It can happen when you experience any negative event, including the loss of a job, a bad interview, failing a test, not being accepted by your peers or colleagues, divorce, separation, and the death of someone close to you. The list is endless, but the voices are always the same:

- Told you—you suck!
- You don't have any talent!
- See, you knew you were stupid!
- Nobody wants you!
- I don't know why you applied for that job in the first place.
- You're a loser—and everyone knows it!
- Why would they even want to be around someone like you?
- Of course he left—you're ugly!
- She died to get away from you.

Someone who has never actively experienced negative self-talk would have no concept of how painful it is to hear those words coming from inside themselves. And even though they may think, "Well, just ignore it," *you* know that you *can't* ignore it. How do you ignore something that feeds so much into your anxieties? Depression? Mood disorder? Negative self-talk is all-around bad energy that just gives those mental health conditions more fuel.

Those who struggle with depression, anxiety, and other mood disorders experience chemical imbalances in the brain. It is not something they can control because the problem is, literally, all in their heads! The only way to correct these imbalances is with medication, and even those don't always work. Even though our brains are all made the same way, they don't all function the same way. Each person's brain chemistry is different. In most instances, the differences are very subtle.

But for someone with a mental health condition, the differences are quite noticeable. Because their brains don't have the proper neurochemical balance, they have difficulty ignoring things like negative self-talk. Getting away from negative self-talk isn't about will power or the latest craze designed to help you "find your center." Getting rid of negative self-talk is an active, conscious process that takes not only hard work on the part of the person experiencing it but also patience and understanding from the people in that person's world, along with a skilled and compassionate counselor, therapist, psychiatrist, or other certified mental health care professional.

When you begin the therapeutic process, you may be asked to chronicle the NST that seems to never go away, but how do you ignore voices that sound eerily familiar? Didn't your mom always say you were too ugly to catch a man? Your dad constantly told you that your grades weren't good enough. Your grandparents lavished devotion on your siblings, but you were too "odd" to merit their attention. Your brother always did better in sports, and he lorded it over you. Your "friends" took the most intimate secrets you shared with them and blabbed them all over school to prove you were a gullible loser. Your boss is constantly on your back to do better, better, better, and then he calls you out in front of your coworkers as a hapless mess.

It is clear that the external negative voices we are exposed to can translate into the negative self-talk we are desperate to get away from. Desperation manifests itself because more often than not, those thoughts keep going around and around in your mind and in your ears; it's an endless cycle of self-beratement that you want to stop, but your mind won't let you.

It can be as simple as being reminded of a time when you were lonely because you had no friends, or as complex as physical or mental abuse suffered at the hands of a loved one over a long period of time. If negative self-talk isn't recognized and treated, the results can be disastrous.

It is important to note that NST, when left unchecked, can lead to suicidal ideation, defined by Healthline.com as a preoccupation "with the idea of suicide. You may regularly think about the way you would commit suicide or think about what life would be like if you weren't around. You may also replay the suicidal act out in your mind" (Legg, 2019). If you or someone you know is experiencing suicidal ideation, don't hesitate to reach out for help.

The National Suicide Prevention Lifeline is available 24 hours a day, with operators who speak both

English and Spanish. Call 800-273-8255 for immediate assistance, or get to the nearest emergency room as soon as possible.

Even though some people may say it's "all just talk" or that a person is trying to get attention, suicide is a serious matter, and anyone who talks about it should be taken seriously.

Chapter 2: How the Brain Generates Self-Talk

It is during our darkest moments that we must focus to see the light.

—Aristotle

Let's take Aristotle's timeless advice and focus. We know that our brains are made of blood, fluids, gray matter, white matter, and trillions of neurological cells that communicate through electrical impulses. These transmissions happen by the billions every second of every day to keep the complexities of the human body in homeostasis—a state of balance. The brain controls the body systems, generates energy for thought, and adapts to the ever-changing environment inside the skull. Let's take a quick look at a simple diagram to understand what parts of the brain we will be discussing and how they function:

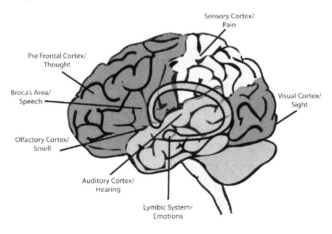

(Sword and Zimbardo, 2014)

The diagram gives us a sense of the major regions of the brain. We can clearly see that thought is produced in the prefrontal cortex (PFC). This is where the information from the other regions of the brain comes together to form thoughts. The PFC gathers information on pain (sensory cortex), speech (Broca's area), smells (olfactory cortex), sights (visual cortex), and sounds (auditory cortex). When particular emotions are associated with this information, those are found in the limbic system near the center of the brain.

So how does the brain corral all that information and combine it to make thoughts? Researchers Steven Frankland and Joshua Greene, at Harvard University, have suggested that "according to one theory, the brain does it by representing conceptual variables, answers to recurring questions of meaning such as 'What was done?' and 'Who did it?' and 'To whom was it done?' A new thought such as 'Biden beats Putin' can then be built by making 'beating' the value of the action variable, 'Biden' the value of the 'agent' variable (Who did it?), and 'Putin' the value of the 'patient' variable (To whom was it done?)." Frankland and Greene are the first brain researchers to point to specific regions of the brain that encode such mental syntax—that is, create thoughts (Reuell, 2015).

Through these types of symbols and operations that are similar to mathematical algorithms, the brain constructs thoughts. Our brains recognize symbols that are used over and over and "we find that the structure of the thought is mapped onto the structure of the brain in a systematic way" (Reuell, 2015). When our brain takes in information, it combines the sensory information with our learned experiences and past memories to form new thoughts. If those thoughts are positive, we generate self-talk that reminds us how wonderful

14

something was, or how much we loved someone or something.

If those thoughts are made up of negative memories and feelings, we generate self-talk that picks at our confidence and reminds us about tragedy, trauma, bullying, or even death. Negative self-talk is driven primarily by the negative emotions and experiences that are poured into the thought process.

The symbols the brain uses can be simple or complex, and they are often repetitive. NST doesn't have to work hard to find those negative nuggets of despair and demoralization that make no effort whatsoever to hide amongst the other thoughts of the brain. They stand out—bright and proud and strong—because they are tied to meaningful relationships and people in our lives.

Sometimes, the bright red blinking of negative self-talk can run roughshod over the pure, white lights of pleasant memories and happy times. This is one of the mechanisms we need to work on when we decide to challenge our negative self-talk, along with classifying memories, learning to consciously choose, and learning to say no to NST.

That leaves us with a challenge. If self-talk is based on the formation of thoughts, and thoughts are formed through a process we cannot control, how can we recognize what is happening, let alone do anything about it?

Chapter 3: How to Recognize the Negative Voice

Many people who struggle with negative self-talk have no clue it is even happening. They don't realize it is a product of their own minds created by memories, symbols, and emotions. They don't even realize they are talking to themselves. All they know is that they feel bad, sad, frustrated, sorrowful, pitiful, or downright useless. And they don't think there is anything anyone can do to help them. They have no hope. They don't recognize that NST is toxic.

Basically, negative self-talk is any inner dialogue you have with yourself that may be limiting your ability to believe in yourself and your own abilities, and to reach your potential. It is any thought that diminishes your ability to make positive changes in your life or your confidence in yourself to do so. So negative self-talk can not only be stressful, but it can really stunt your success. NST can affect us in some pretty damaging ways. One large-scale study found that rumination and self-blame over negative events were linked to an increased risk of mental health problems. Focusing on negative thoughts may lead to decreased motivation as well as greater feelings of helplessness. This type of critical inner dialogue has even been linked to depression, so it's definitely something to fix. (Scott, 2020)

Negative self-talk is very damaging and can lead to many problems in day-to-day life. Sometimes, it can lead to things you wouldn't even imagine.

Negative self-talk can lead to a lowered ability to see opportunities, as well as a decreased tendency to capitalize on these opportunities. This means that the heightened sense of stress comes from both the perception and the changes in behavior that come from it. Other consequences of negative self-talk can include:

Limited thinking: The more you tell yourself you can't do something, the more you believe it.

Perfectionism: You begin to really believe that "great" isn't as good as "perfect," and that perfection is actually attainable. In contrast, mere high achievers tend to do better than their perfectionistic counterparts because they are generally less stressed and are happy with a job well done. They don't pick it apart and try to zero in on what could have been better.

Feelings of depression: Some research has shown that negative self-talk can lead to an exacerbation of feelings of depression. If left unchecked, this could be quite damaging.

Relationship challenges: Whether the constant self-criticism makes you seem needy and insecure or you turn your negative self-talk into more general negative habits that bother others, a lack of communication and even a "playful" amount of criticism can take a toll.

One of the most obvious drawbacks of negative self-talk is that it's not positive. This sounds simplistic, but research has shown that positive self-talk is a great predictor of success. (Scott, 2020)

For someone who is feeling desperate and depressed with relationship issues and has a seemingly bleak future, it is essential to seek medical help, particularly if suicidal ideation is present. Mental health care professionals—psychologists, psychiatrists, therapists, and counselors—and primary care physicians can recognize when the symptoms of NST have reached a dangerous level and help the patient find appropriate resources.

However, let's say you are reading this book because you've "done therapy" and it didn't help with NST. We are glad you are still trying to help yourself, and we commend you.

Close your eyes for a moment. Drown out the chatter and noise of the room. Focus on your breathing. After taking three deep breaths, open your eyes and identify your very first thought. If it is negative self-talk, it's time to take steps to recognize that negative voice when it starts drowning out the chatter of everyday life, or the peaceful silence of meditation.

Write It Down

Journaling is one of the cornerstones of modern therapeutic techniques. As Dr. Phil says quite often, "We can't change something we don't acknowledge" (2002–present).

He's not wrong. It is not unusual for patients who need mental health help to avoid journaling. Why? Because once you write it down, *it's real*. It cannot be shoved back into a box.

It cannot be ignored. It cannot be brushed off. Once it's real, you *have* to deal with it, and that can be very painful.

As a matter of survival, humans recoil from pain. If we brush up against a hot stove or accidentally walk on a tack, the pain receptors in the various parts of our bodies send warning signals to the brain that it's time to back off and assess for injury. We do this automatically. Think about it - if you step on something sharp, what is the first thing you do? You look at the bottom of your foot. You assess the damage. You take the necessary steps to start the healing process. Then you figure out what caused the pain. If it's a silly ole tack, you may yell at it, call it names, and then throw it away. And you will probably never think about the incident again—ever. It's not the same with negative self-talk.

Somewhere in our prefrontal cortex, negative self-talk is doing one of two things: actively badgering you around the clock, or waiting for the perfect moment to strike! Either way, NST brings pain. But how do we step back when the source of our pain is inside our own heads? We can't. That's the biggest realization people need to understand: you cannot physically escape negative self-talk.

You can't just throw NST in the trash can or put ointment on it to soothe the pain. If you try to shove it deeper into the recesses of your mind, praying it will get lost and never find its way out again, you are hoping in vain. NST leaves breadcrumbs in the shape of memories and sounds of voices that can never truly be hidden away in the mind. The pain associated with negative self-talk has to be experienced before you can deal with it. Yes, *you will need to feel* the embarrassment, the humiliation, the abuse, the anger, the disbelief, the sadness, the hurt, and so much more before you can begin your journey to defeat negative self-talk.

Lila's Story

Lila grew up overweight and was constantly bullied for her size and belittled for her looks. In adulthood, she found that she never wanted to go out with friends or do any activities that involved strangers or crowds. Why? She knew that if she was exposed to strangers, they would mock her relentlessly and make fun of her appearance. That is what her negative self-talk told her. It was the only way she had ever interacted with others in social situations. There was no upside to her leaving the house.

Lila was also a talented writer. She had been writing poems and stories since she was eight years old. She read hundreds of books, increasing her vocabulary, and strengthening her intelligence. She studied hard in school, eventually earning two college degrees. Yet no one ever gave her praise for her accomplishments. Her parents concerned themselves with why she didn't have a boyfriend and how her degrees in English were worthless in the "real world." Her friends were jealous of her mind and tore her down with subtle slights.

Though she wrote in a journal often, she never wrote about her negative self-talk. She didn't want to acknowledge that there were these random, hurtful, damaging thoughts destroying her one day at a time. It wasn't until she attempted suicide that anyone took her seriously.

You see, Lila hid her depression and all the pain she was in by trying to make people laugh and by trying to be the best at whatever she did. Her negative self-talk told her that no one wanted her, she was fat and ugly, and her parents were incredibly disappointed that she wasted her time in college. This young woman had nothing positive in her life—nothing.

But she kept going on, trying to make a difference, trying to be a good friend and daughter. The pressure finally got to her, and she listened when her NST finally said, "Just end it," for the millionth time.

After being treated at the hospital for her suicide attempt, Lila began therapy. Her therapist helped her understand that the "little voice" was just all her anger and emotions trying to express themselves. But she didn't want to acknowledge them, so she pushed them back over and over and over again—to no avail. The therapist encouraged her to use her writing as a therapeutic device. Lila had to sit down and write any time she heard the "little voice." She had to write about what it said, who it sounded like, and what it reminded her of.

This process was incredibly painful. Every time Lila sat down to journal, she wept. She felt the hurt and anger and frustration and disappointment she had been pushing away all of her life. She was now actually *feeling* those things from the past that she didn't want to. She had thought herself clever: "If I don't feel them, I won't be hurt." She could not have been more wrong. She never realized that if she was going to stop the negative self-talk and really heal, she had to experience the pain of the past and then let it go.

Some people might think, How could you *not* let it go? You've experienced awful, painful things! There are two things here that people don't consider. One is that going through pain is *terrible*. When you reach into the depths of your mind and soul and release pain, you feel it in every single cell of your body and every part of your soul. It's like a flood that keeps you underwater and you can't breathe. The second is that when you've spent years believing certain things about yourself, letting them go can be scary. If you aren't who you always thought you were, then who are you? How can I start over if this huge part of who I am is gone? Do I really have to feel this pain and change my core? Yes, it is vital if you hope to recover from negative self-talk.

No matter what the cause, emotional pain can be intense and significantly affect many different areas of your life. While it is often dismissed as being less serious than physical pain, it is important that emotional pain is taken seriously. There are a number of common feelings that are associated with emotional pain that can have an impact on both your physical and mental health.

- Deep sorrow, sadness, or depression
- Grief
- Intense distress
- Loneliness and isolation
- Negative emotions
- Panic
- Rage
- Shame
- Worthlessness

In some cases, feelings of emotional pain may lead to physical symptoms that do not have an identifiable physical cause. Treatment for emotional pain often involves addressing the underlying source of the symptoms, so treatment often depends upon the individual diagnosis. (Hartney, 2020)

It requires incredible bravery and strength to take these steps. Sometimes, it is helpful to approach these things with a therapist so that you have immediate comfort and support. A therapist can help you through the pain and ride the waves with you. Then they can help you redefine your life, using only the positive things that remain.

By facing the NST head on, Lila was finally able to see all she had accomplished in her life, *despite* the negative people around her. She was able to celebrate her survival. And now she had some names for the "little voice," like Mom, Dad, Julie, Dean, Jaime, and so many others. She had finally identified the voice.

Identify the Voice

Once you acknowledge the existence of the negative self-talk voice, identify its owner. Who is talking? Who does the voice sound like? Why does that particular voice talk about that particular thing? And why are these words—these abstract, non-corporeal things—painful?

Because we tend to believe them—their presence is very strong. "Emotional pain can often feel as strong as physical pain and at times can even cause symptoms of pain throughout the body. It can also have a detrimental impact on both short-term and long-term mental well-being . . . Because emotional pain can be so distressing, people often turn to unhealthy coping mechanisms, including drugs and alcohol. The problem is that while these methods might provide short-term relief, they cause greater damage in the long run" (Hartney, 2021).

Rosie's Story

Rosie, who grew up with a judgmental mother, may always have a voice in her ear saying that she needs to "go on a diet" or do better with putting on makeup. Imagine you are an 11-year-old girl and you've had a growth spurt. You grew five inches over the summer. You also gained weight, but since you spent every moment outside running, biking, swimming, and playing sports, you've put on quite a bit of muscle too. Rosie is a tomboy, and she likes it that way.

However, her mother is a country club debutante who can't believe her only little girl won't wear fancy dresses or go to tea service with her mother and grandmother. Why is her darling angel outside getting all dirty and playing with those boys? Imagine being subjected to constant humiliation and ridicule as your mother tries to explain your appearance and actions to her highfalutin friends:

- "Oh, she's just going through a phase."
- "She loves music too and can sing like an angel!"
- "Honey, you are so much better looking in girls' clothes."
- "Sweetie, you can't get a husband if you act like a boy."
- "It's time you start learning how to act like a young lady, not a tomboy."

These judgments and criticisms all do the same thing: invalidate the feelings and even the existence of a young girl who simply isn't a girly girl.

When those who are closest to us invalidate our very existence, it is hard to accept. Rosie doesn't feel loved or encouraged or valued. All Rosie will remember is the constant badgering by her mother to conform to some standard that she has no desire to achieve. She will grow up thinking to herself, "My mother doesn't love me because I am different."

Fifteen years later, this badgered and bullied girl has become a college graduate and is working in a job she loves—finance. Despite being a woman in a "man's game," she is hugely successful and has a gorgeous house and many good friends. She is admired and respected by her superiors and colleagues. She also coaches girls' basketball as a volunteer and enjoys every minute of it. Her girls look up to her as an example of a successful woman, and she encourages them to strive and achieve because they can be anything they want. But what runs through Rosie's head in the morning when she looks in the mirror?

- "Your makeup is terrible."
- "You certainly can't put together an outfit."
- "Why would you want to get all stinky running around a basketball court?"
- "You haven't found a boyfriend yet, have you?"
- "Why did you have to work in finance? Couldn't you just get married? Be a teacher?"

Rosie can't stop hearing these negative thoughts, and she has turned to some pretty nasty coping mechanisms to deal with it. Even though she is still doing great at her job and working with the kids, at home, in secret, she downs a bottle of wine every night to try and drown out the voices so she can sleep. While she may be functioning now, it won't be long before her alcohol abuse takes a toll on her, in every aspect of her life.

A parent's expectations are a fertile breeding ground for the basis of negative self-talk. In particular, the relationship with the parent of the same gender is crucial to a youngster developing their own personality, desires, and goals—and seeking approval. Many of the most driven, successful people in this world are that way simply because they are either trying to meet impossible expectations or trying to prove that they can be whatever they want *despite* expectations. Short of cutting a parent out of one's life, the digs and scratches that end up manifesting themselves as negative self-talk will remain until they are recognized.

What if that voice sounds exactly like your bully from high school, the one who *never* gave you a moment's peace? If you were chunky, really smart, wore glasses, were in band, sang in choir, or had any other quality that made you "different," there was never a dearth of bullies available to remind you of your shortcomings.

> Research shows that the effects of bullying last well into adulthood. In fact, one study found that the consequences of being bullied by peers may have a greater impact on mental health in adulthood than originally thought. What's more, the impact may be even more significant than being mistreated by adults. Remember, the experiences that people have while they are children help mold them into the adults that they later become. So it is not surprising that the effects of bullying linger well into adulthood. This then helps to influence their future mindset, including how they view themselves and others. (Gordon, 2020)

In essence, as adults, we hang onto the voices of those childhood and adolescent bullies in the form of negative self-talk, as Brian can attest to.

Brian's Story

Brian was a quiet, brilliant mind. He excelled in all his classes, but particularly in photography and journalism. One would think that would bring him recognition from his peers, and from some it did. But there will always be someone out there you threaten with your talent. Yes, most people who are bullied are a *threat* to the bully.

Brian had few friends outside of the A/V club and journalism classes. He was called names all the time like "faggot" and "nerd" and "idiot." More than once, bullies shoved him against lockers, tried to steal his camera equipment, or tripped him in the cafeteria so that his lunch spilled everywhere. It got so bad that Brian created a path for himself—how he could get to his classes while avoiding the bullies. Sometimes it worked, and those were Brian's good days. But most times, he couldn't escape the torture.

Brian tried desperately to focus on his schoolwork and practice his photography. He had a great, supportive family, but his lack of friends—people who could insulate him at school or stand up for him—made every day at school very difficult. Brian was so genuinely afraid of his classmates that he skipped graduation ceremonies. He was afraid to be with all of them on the stage since it would put him in a very vulnerable position.

When Brian started college, in a program for gifted artists, he found himself among true peers for the first time. Everyone in his classes had gone through similar bullying in high school and understood what it was like. His first day with his new peers was amazing!

But negative self-talk has a way of sneaking up on you. When his first big project was due, Brian was nervous. He set up his display for his presentation and turned to his classmates to begin. He knew his material and was proud of his work, but all he heard in his head was this: "You're still a faggot!" "Art is for weaklings—and you're an idiot!" He stumbled over his introduction, and the voices played on in his mind all the way to the end of his presentation. But his classmates could almost see what was happening in his mind by the look on his face. They all knew that look intimately. To show their support, no one snickered, or chortled, or made fun of Brian's work. They sincerely applauded him after his presentation.

After class, his professor asked him to stay. Brian knew his voices were right: he was an idiot. But the professor was kind and compassionate and could tell that something was wrong. When he asked Brian what happened during his presentation, Brian tried to brush it off as just being nervous. But the professor knew that wasn't the case, and he gently prodded Brian to open up and share what was bothering him.

Brian finally started sobbing and told the professor about all the bullying and how the voices always seemed to drag him down during his most important moments. The professor didn't mock Brian or tease him for crying. He reminded Brian that those days were past, and that Brian was in a different environment where he had already earned everyone's respect and admiration with his talent. He also reminded Brian that artists are a powerful force, and bullies can't live up to that.

Keep in mind that bullies are generally insecure people trying to raise themselves up to a standard they are desperate to meet. Did you ever realize that? Bullies are desperate people too. Does that mean we should feel sorry for them? Not necessarily. But if we can acknowledge that they are in just as much pain as we are, it can help silence the negative self-talk. You can acknowledge that their voices come from the same source of pain that yours come from. They are struggling too.

Acknowledge the Problem

So now you know who the negative self-talk originated from. What next? You need to take a deep breath, gather your courage, and acknowledge the source.

Any time you have one of those thoughts, stop what you are doing and close your eyes. Imagine the person behind the voice. Acknowledge that the problem exists because of past words and actions that the person didn't realize were incredibly painful and demeaning, not from anything going on in the present. "While it may be painful to think about the bullying you experienced as a kid, if it is still impacting your everyday life and the way you view yourself, then it is best to face the issue head-on. Once you have come to terms with what you experienced and changed the way you view yourself and others, you will be on your way to recovery" (Gordon, 2020).

Most people go through life not realizing that their behaviors and words have an effect on any number of people around them. For those who seek to inspire, their words and actions will be a positive influence on everyone they meet. These inspired leaders want only to see the best in people, recognize their talents, and encourage them to go for their dreams. Inspirational leaders are most often the birth of positive self-talk.

What about that person who is the source of negative self-talk? Do you think they are being intentionally destructive? In some cases, yes, they are because they don't know any other way to be. It is clear that those who inflict pain may simply know no other way to behave. They grew up being abused or belittled, so that's the only way they know how to behave. Most people from older generations didn't seek help or go to therapy because it wasn't considered "normal." They lived by the "suck it up" rule—it's a jungle out there and only the strong survive.

"Boomers grew up in an era when mental health issues where not discussed, much less acknowledged. Conditions such as anorexia, bulimia, ADHD, PTSD, autism, and learning disabilities were unheard of and depression and anxiety were viewed as signs of weakness. Boomers were, and are, accustomed to toughing things out and not asking for help when things get difficult (Work, 2021).

"But their attitudes toward mental toughness do not make them immune to mental illnesses. Current statistics show that 25 percent of people over 55 experience some form of mental health issue, but many go undiagnosed or untreated (especially men). The most common mental health issues for people over 50 are:

- Depression. Risk factors include chronic physical illness and/or pain, diminishing physical functioning, grief and loss, and medications.
- Anxiety disorders. Traumatic events, social isolation, medical issues, financial concerns and/or impaired memory can increase anxiety in older adults.

- Dementia. Age, high blood pressure, diabetes, strokes, sedentary lifestyle, head injury, and alcohol abuse are all factors in the development of dementia. After 65, the likelihood of developing some form of dementia increases every five years and by age 85, more than 50 percent of people are affected" (Work, 2021).

It's clear that the baby boomer generation had a very different upbringing than recent generations, and that baby boomers are reluctant to get help for anything at all. Since it's how they grew up, in their own way, they may have been trying to make you strong. But their technique was ultimately destructive. Can you acknowledge how much pain they are still causing you? Why are those hurtful memories always the first thing to come to mind? Usually, it's because that person who tore us down and continues to make us feel insufficient is someone we love and respect.

Can you forgive them? Can you find a way to say, "Okay, *you* screwed up, not me. I don't have to listen to you anymore. You have no place in my life, NST"? Assign those thoughts to a new source—negative self-talk. When you consciously disconnect the person from the NST, it is easier to recognize it for what it is: a collection of thoughts and memories triggered by a stimulus you just experienced.

One way to acknowledge the problem is to seek counseling. Later, we will talk about different ways you can get help for your negative self-talk. But many people, like our friend Darcy, are afraid to go to therapy because it is just one more thing that people can belittle her for.

"What? Are you so weak that you have to have a therapist tell you how to fix what's wrong with you?" "Why aren't you strong enough to handle it on your own?" "Don't you realize it's just your imagination?"

Here is an important truth: **seeking help is not a sign of weakness; it is a sign of strength!** "Most people who have grown up in individualistic cultures like the United States are often raised with the belief that relying on others and asking for help is a burden to others and makes you seem emotionally weak. Despite these views, there is ultimately very little that any of us do to succeed fully on our own, even if that is hard to acknowledge. You need both independence and dependence—not one or the other. Our need to be alone and to pursue our individual goals must be balanced with our need to be with others, and when necessary, to request help" (Rosenberg, 2019).

A weak person will continue to allow NST to dominate his or her life and drown in the negativity until they cannot take it anymore. A strong person determines that this is too much for a single person to bear and the only way to get better is to have someone help you untangle the mess that your mind has become. It's great to be able to go to friends or family for support when this is your truth. But those who are invested in us personally can't always give themselves the emotional distance required to help us fully. Sometimes, only an outsider—like a therapist—can help you figure out the core of your NST and the memories and moments you need to address directly to escape from their grasp.

A good therapist will tell you that suppression of negative self-talk is no solution. "To send it packing for good, you need to cultivate the skills of awareness, labeling, distraction, replacement, reframing, and gratitude" (Genomind, 2019). These are skills you most definitely can pick up in therapy. Those who are successful in therapy "learn to acknowledge and observe their mental activity <u>without automatically accepting the unpleasant thoughts as true or relevant</u>. Their refusal to identify with negative feelings helps strip those feelings of their psychological power" (Genomind, 2019).

Another thing that gets in your way of moving forward is emotional agony, a psychological and physiological condition that feeds into negative self-talk. "Emotional agony tends to affect and change the whole person, from our values and outlook on life to how we treat others. Learning how to recognize agony and its effects can help you channel those changes in a more positive direction . . . Most everyone experiences the emotional pain of rejection or failure at some point in their life. However, for some, the feeling of rejection can lead to a persistent feeling of emotional agony that is chronic and ongoing" (James, 2021). Sound familiar? Sounds like a pretty accurate description of negative self-talk to me.

Once you have identified how your brain works, what's going on when you form a thought, and how you can recognize the sources of your negative self-talk, you need to take some time to identify all the bad actors of NST that pop into your mind and confront them, one by one. It will be painful and challenging. It will make you emotional and doubtful. Facing one's demons is never going to be easy, but if you don't, you will forever be their victim, not the person you know you are and who you know you can be.

The man who moves a mountain begins by carrying away small stones.

—Confucius

Part II: Identify and Confront

Our brains never sleep—even when we sleep! In fact, during sleep is when our brains perform a daily "reboot" of our systems. When we deny ourselves sleep, we can't form or maintain the neural pathways in the brain that allow us to learn and generate new memories.

Sleep is critical for all brain functions, including how neurons communicate with each other. Would it surprise you to know that your brain is remarkably active as you sleep? Scientific findings suggest that during sleep, the brain "takes out the trash" by removing toxins that build up during your waking hours (National, 2019).

So why is there no "trash man" for our negative thoughts, memories, and emotions? Those things are just as harmful to our well-being as chemical toxins or other by-products that our bodies produce. The answer is actually quite simple: our brain is a computer. Computers don't have emotions; they can only process and categorize them. The word "negative" is an association that something is bad or painful. Our brain processes don't recognize any memory or thought or self-talk as either positive or negative.

This is one of the great mysteries of the mind: we connect emotionally with images, thoughts, and other sensory information, but the electrical impulses that send information between neurons aren't emotional in nature.

Remember our picture of the brain? Emotions are formed in the limbic region, one of the smallest parts of the brain. The majority of our brain power is devoted to keeping us alive through our organ systems and helping us learn as we encounter new experiences and activities.

Perhaps that is why self-talk happens in the first place. Our brains are too busy doing higher-order functions to bother with something like self-talk. Just like any other computer, the brain only has so much space to give to each function. And those lower-order functions are things that seep into our consciousness and that we have to deal with. Self-talk in general is primarily an unconscious process, and both conscious and unconscious processes start in the limbic region of the brain:

> The limbic system acts as *a control center for conscious and unconscious functions*, regulating much of what the body does. In some ways, it connects the mind to the body, bridging the gap between psychological and physiological experiences . . . Both the amygdala and hippocampus (two parts of the limbic system) help the brain form new memories, store those memories, retrieve them, and *make sense of their emotional content*. The limbic system is dynamic, changing with input from a person's environment. Experience changes this important brain region, and that may help explain why people's psychological and physiological experiences change over time. Therapy, too, may change the limbic system by training the brain to process information differently. (Villines, 2019)

So by the time we wake up in the morning, our limbic system has processed all of our experiences and memories and emotions from the day before, placing them in storage. Knowing that the freshly woken brain is at its peak, it seems like when we first wake would be the optimal time to consider what thoughts our brains are currently producing and whether or not we need to engage with those thoughts, dismiss them, or fight them. Do we participate in self-talk (positive or negative) or do we try to focus our thoughts on the day ahead?

If we can identify our negative self-talk, categorize it even, we have taken our first step toward defeating it. According to Sparks (2019), ". . . common forms of negative self-talk include:

> Filtering: You magnify the negative aspects of a situation and filter out all of the positive ones. For example, you had a great day at work. You completed your tasks ahead of time and were complimented for doing a speedy and thorough job. That evening, you focus only on your plan to do even more tasks and forget about the compliments you received.
>
> Personalizing: When something bad occurs, you automatically blame yourself. For example, you hear that an evening out with friends is canceled, and you assume that the change in plans is because no one wanted to be around you.
>
> Catastrophizing: You automatically anticipate the worst. The drive-through coffee shop gets your order wrong, and you automatically think that the rest of your day will be a disaster.
>
> Polarizing: You see things only as either good or bad. There is no middle ground. You feel that you have to be perfect or you're a total failure."

It is easy to see how the forms of negative self-talk could overtake our thinking and ruin our day. But is there harm in ignoring self-talk? Maybe, maybe not. The experts certainly have opinions on it: "The thoughts that rumble through your head—the ones inciting anger over what someone did to you, depressing you about what you can't control, igniting and incensing your ethical sense over the cruelty and disregard of others—aren't helping you. You might believe you are entitled to the negative self-talk. You might actually enjoy wallowing in it sometimes in order to justify and confirm you are right, but it gives you nothing and takes so much of your life away.

"Negative self-talk doesn't just stay in your mind; it often leads to actions you might sometimes regret. It might encourage you to 'tell that other person off,' or 'refuse to be taken advantage of,' or 'quit this stupid boss,' or it might lead to a destructive relationship, or a breakdown in family relations, or isolating yourself from a long-time friend or relative because it helps you to justify that this is the right thing to do. Maybe it's to protect yourself, maybe to get justice, or maybe just because the pain of the negative self-talk is so deep you just simply have to do something" (Flaxington, 2020).

Flaxington makes the point that while negative self-talk can be something people choose to "wallow" in, it is clearly unhealthy to simply ignore it. NST can lead to negative actions in your daily life that you won't be able to take back.

Scientists in the past two decades have begun to refer to negative self-talk as negative self-referent thoughts. They have clearly determined that ignoring NST can have an extremely negative effect on a person's well-being. Researchers have found that thought suppression (ignoring) is a factor in the origin and continuance of "a variety of psychological disorders, including obsessive-compulsive disorder, post-traumatic stress disorder, and depression . . . In the current study, we examined the effects of suppressing negative self-referent thoughts on self-esteem and mood. Participants who suppressed their negative thoughts, compared to those who did not, experienced lower self-esteem and more anxious and depressed mood. In addition, participants who rated their thoughts as highly depressing were particularly vulnerable to the negative effects of suppression. The results emphasize the importance of examining the consequences to the self-concept and mood of suppressing negative self-referent thoughts" (Borton et al., 2005).

It seems obvious that experts agree that ignoring negative self-talk can be self-destructive. That is why it is critical to learn how to define both positive and negative self-talk that you experience.

Chapter 4: Defining the Positive and Negative Self-Talk

The phenomenon of self-talk has been recognized by the psychiatric community as a genuine experience of the mind. "Our self-talk can be cheerful and supportive or negative and self-defeating. Self-talk can be beneficial when it's positive, calming fears and bolstering confidence. Human nature, unfortunately, is prone to negative self-talk, including sweeping assertions like 'I can't do anything right' or 'I'm a complete failure'" ("Self-Talk," 2021).

In order to properly define your self-talk as positive or negative, you first have to acknowledge its existence. It happens. It's real. It doesn't mean you are going crazy. It doesn't mean you *are* crazy. This is something that happens to *everyone*. It is a biochemical reaction to outside stimulus. That's all. What makes it complicated is what we do with it when it happens.

Positive self-talk is generally easy to identify. Athletes call it "getting psyched up" before a big game. Actors and artists call it "finding the muse." However people choose to define it, positive self-talk is all about encouragement, confidence, and improving performance. It is something we actually encourage among students, giving them "pep talks" and hoping they remember what nuggets of wisdom we gave them when the time comes. Additionally, it's true that "some people believe they can credit their success to having a strong inner voice. In some cases, even a critical inner voice can push individuals to achieve by raising awareness of internal and external obstacles to achievement" ("Self-Talk," 2021).

It's one thing to have a "critical inner voice"—one that examines your mistakes and reminds you not to do that again, but negative self-talk is more damaging.

Negative self-talk is another creature entirely. If you are aware of it, you might call it "putting yourself down" or "not taking credit." Those who can recognize it easily can just as easily dismiss it. But for those whose past experiences are fraught with trauma, NST sounds too much like what they know, and they cannot differentiate between destructive words from the past and the truth of the reality in front of them. This is the main difference between positive and negative self-talk. Positive self-talk drives someone to achieve and succeed at what they are doing in the moment. Negative self-talk takes a person to the *past* and dredges up negative emotions and experiences that can paralyze them with fear, self-loathing, or anger.

"Research finds that when self-talk focuses on the present moment instead, and on seeing that moment and its opportunities as valuable, it more effectively helps us reach our goals" ("Self-Talk," 2021). It's clear that one of the most effective strategies for handling negative self-talk is to keep your mind and thoughts in the present and not dwell on negative incidents of the past.

"Rarely is dwelling on the past seen in a positive light. Nor should it be. Thinking too much about times gone by typically keeps your mind—and life—stuck in neutral (and maybe even shifts it into reverse). If you habitually ruminate over your earlier life, you may regularly be revisited by feelings of anger, guilt, resentment, sorrow, or shame. And such emotions are hardly productive. In many ways, they're downright toxic. Fretfully obsessing about the people and events precipitating such negative feelings can lead to endless recycling. If you become increasingly stagnant . . . your thinking really can't progress toward any adaptive resolution" (Seltzer, 2011).

Since negative self-talk is most often attached to events from the past, it is sometimes hard to move forward because you have to try and forget the past.

Kia's Story

Kia grew up with a terrific family. She had a stay-at-home mom and a hard-working father, as well as siblings, grandparents, aunts, uncles, and cousins galore. There was always something going on. They went with their parents and other family members to the softball diamond on the weekends, ate hot dogs, had cotton candy, and enjoyed playing catch just outside the dugouts. They were together with family every holiday and birthday, or whenever an occasion called for it. But Kia had some strange behavioral tics that made her cousins and siblings tease her relentlessly—to the point that she spent a lot of her childhood running to her mother, crying about the other kids being mean, and then sitting at her mother's side until it was time to go home.

What Kia didn't know, and what she wouldn't know until she was in her late 40s, was that she had Asperger's syndrome. When she was growing up, people with mental health issues were separated from society and put into "homes," and they were never seen again. Her family simply found her behavior to be immature and childish. She was constantly told to "grow up" or "I'll give you something to really cry about." What they didn't know was that Kia couldn't process the input from social situations. She couldn't see the gray area in things. If a neighborhood child was mean to her,

41

that meant all children were mean. But if her grandmother loved her, then all grandmothers loved her.

Kia couldn't understand why she couldn't have her way all the time. Her way, in her mind, was always better. And while that may have been true upon occasion, nobody likes a know-it-all. The other children used Kia when it was convenient, such as studying for a test (like many children with autism spectrum disorder, Kia was extremely bright), but nagged her and called her names the rest of the time for their own amusement.

Kia struggled to get along with others her whole childhood, her entire adolescence, and well into her 20s. She almost got arrested when she was 23 because she followed a man she liked into a club and then trailed him around the club like a puppy. He was irritated and exhausted—he didn't like her—and he finally confronted her directly and told her to leave him alone or he would call the cops. Kia was devastated. Why didn't he see that she just wanted to get to know him, and she had to spend time with him for that! For months after, Kia ran from any man she felt slightly attracted to because all she heard in her head was the following: "I'm gonna call the cops!"

Years later, and thousands of hours of therapy later, Kia learned to define all of her negative self-talk; how it related to her ASD behavior; and how, no matter what, she was a good person who was funny, smart, and loving to everyone she knew. She became a great leader in her community, tutored children, donated to the poor, and was almost always available if someone needed a hand. Though Kia suffered for years with no answers, she was finally able to move forward with her future.

Do you really want to stay stuck in the gooey mire of the negative past? Ask yourself this question: Would I wish this on anyone? The answer is always going to be no. So why is it okay to do it to yourself? It may be because you were never supported or given the confidence to stand up for yourself. It is true that the hardest person to stand up to is *yourself*! Lacking the courage to do so can allow the negative self-talk to continually invade our thoughts.

Chapter 5: What Leads Us to Negative Self-Talk

Negative self-talk comes from various places, but it can always be found in trauma survivors, people who were abused or bullied, people with severe anxiety, people with chronic depression, and people who have been diagnosed with mood disorders. As we grow and mature, our brains are growing as well. One of the last parts of the brain to develop (when we reach our early 20s) is the prefrontal cortex—the reasoning and thought-producing center.

Imagine your young PFC being inundated with negativity, abuse, trauma, or even improper brain chemistry for *years* before it reaches full maturity. That's like trying to teach someone with no ears how to hear. The PFC can't respond to the stimulus with any ability to decipher and separate those voices or ideas that are simply nonsense from the voices of reason. It just takes in the information, stores it, and refers back to it when thoughts are produced, including negative self-talk. It has no defense mechanism. The PFC is only there at that time to accept and categorize information gathered by the five senses.

Not only that, but the emotional center of the brain also explodes in adolescence. So not only is the PFC constantly being loaded down with negativity and bad memories, but during adolescence, emotions are running wild across the landscape of the brain, further complicating the imprinting of memories, both good and bad.

To complicate matters, "People with depression and anxiety frequently experience destructive and dysfunctional self-talk; the internal chatter they hear may be incessant and overly critical. Overwhelmed by the negativity, they can wallow in painful rumination, attacking themselves ceaselessly" ("Self-Talk," 2021). Depression and anxiety most commonly show up during adolescence. Worse still is that most teens don't have the reasoning skills to understand that their problem is a medical one, and they rarely seek help. They are far more likely to turn to drugs and alcohol than a psychiatrist or therapist. They, more often than not, attribute the "little voice" as a sign that they are going crazy.

In some cases, because of the lack of reasoning skills in children, older siblings or cousins can control the younger children by abusing their position of authority and capitalizing on their sibling's or cousin's love for them. While this "sibling rivalry" or "friendly teasing" is often dismissed—or entirely missed—by adults, the long-term consequences can be severe.

Robbie's Story

Robbie had a great childhood. He had loving parents, a huge extended family nearby, and two big sisters. While he was growing up, his sisters were often asked to babysit. Since Robbie was significantly younger, the girls convinced him to do things that could be dangerous—for example, eat worms and stick forks in light sockets—and because he loved them so much, he would do anything they requested. His PFC couldn't reason out that these were things he shouldn't be doing. He was just following instructions.

As Robbie entered adolescence and came to understand the torture his sisters put him through, he became preoccupied with risky behaviors. The negative self-talk in his mind had the voice of his sweet sisters telling him that if he didn't do something, he was a "pansy" or a "wuss." He would try anything. It wasn't until he broke his arm after jumping off the roof that his parents finally took note of his reckless behavior, which more often than not was brought on by his negative self-talk "making suggestions."

When confronted by his parents about his behavior, Robbie explained that his sisters had told him over and over that such behaviors were "normal" for a kid and that he shouldn't fear getting into trouble. His parents were furious with his sisters and intended to punish them, but Robbie begged them not to. He was so desperate to hold onto his sisters' love that he couldn't bear the thought of them being punished for something his NST told him to do.

It took months of family therapy for the siblings to come to a rational understanding of healthy relationships, and Robbie soon learned that his negative self-talk was the origin of his risky behaviors. His mind just wanted to continue with the stunts to make his sisters love him. The frequent absence of the parents put Robbie's sisters in the optimal position to take advantage of his love.

It's unfortunate that many parents in today's society are so busy and distracted that they rarely notice there is even a problem with their teen. Friends, teachers, coaches, or counselors are far more likely to note there is a problem than parents. And for any adolescent dealing with negative self-talk, sometimes it's just easier to try to negotiate with the NST than it is to approach a parent or authority figure with the notion that the "little voices are being so mean to me."

It's also been discussed by specialists that the prefrontal cortex development is still occurring in adolescence and underdeveloped functions can lead to risky behavior:

The prefrontal cortex coordinates higher-order cognitive processes and executive functioning. Executive functions are a set of supervisory cognitive skills needed for goal-directed behavior, including planning, response inhibition, working memory, and attention. These skills allow an individual to pause long enough to take stock of a situation, assess his or her options, plan a course of action, and execute it. Poor executive functioning leads to difficulty with planning, attention, using feedback, and mental inflexibility, all of which could undermine judgment and decision making. (Johnson et al., 2009)

Clearly, negative self-talk can be a bad actor when an adolescent's brain is in this stage of development. This can lead to changes in neural pathways and loss of dendrite connections that can stunt the growth in the PFC (Johnson et al., 2009).

When NST runs rampant through adolescence, as the brain matures, the adult who emerges can still be bogged down by it.

"Whether you witnessed or experienced violence as a child or your caretakers emotionally or physically neglected you, when you grow up in a traumatizing environment you are likely to still show signs of that trauma as an adult. Children make meaning out of the events they witness and the things that happen to them, and they create an internal map of how the world is. This meaning-making helps them cope. But if children don't create a new internal map as they grow up, their old way of interpreting the world can damage their ability to function as adults" (Brandt, 2017).

It is essential that a teen with NST seek treatment; otherwise, the adult that teen becomes will have a stunted executive function growth. If they can't deal with their own NST, how are they going to deal with all of the complexities of being an adult in a world that frowns upon the weak? It is essential that a person struggling with NST learn that the voice is the most powerful weapon in confronting NST.

Confronting the Negative Voices

One of the hardest things we do as people who struggle with negative self-talk is admit the voices are there at all. It's a paradox. We know they're there, we listen to them, we react to them, yet we don't *fight* them.

If there was a hateful person whom you had no respect for standing in front of you and berating you, calling you names, and otherwise shaming you, would you take it, or would you get angry? Most people would be furious! We would defend ourselves, possibly even to the point of physical violence. No one wants his or her integrity impugned or his or her qualifications questioned.

So if we would fight a live bully, why don't we fight the evil little orators that live in our minds? There is a simple answer to this question: those voices tend to sound like people we *do* respect—parents, friends, teachers, coaches, etc. We would hesitate to stand up to one of the people we love and respect, no matter what they were saying.

Our culture tells us to never disrespect our elders or those in positions of authority over us. This deep-seated cultural construct stops us from confronting the NST bullies.

Jim's Story

Jim's family was dysfunctional, to say the least. He grew up in the 1970s when most of the kids he knew had stay-at-home moms. His parents both had to work. As a result, he was in charge of his little brother—a total pain in the butt. But Jim was a gentle soul and let his little brother decide what they would do every day. Even with Jim's generous nature and allowing his little brother to take advantage of him, his parents never let up.

"What do you mean you skipped rocks on the river? You know you aren't supposed to go there, you moron!"

"Why isn't your guys' homework done before dinner? Outside playing like lazy asses?"

"Why isn't the laundry folded? We told you that had to be done right away after school, dumb---!"

"Clean up this pigsty! You made the mess, you clean it, idiot!"

Jim didn't know what to do. He simply took the abuse and tried to keep his brother out of it. As the big brother, Jim felt it was his responsibility to meet his parents' expectations. It never, ever occurred to him to fight back.

After graduating from high school and starting college, Jim quickly got engaged to his first girlfriend. Years later, he confided in a friend that his wife was so much like his mother that he wondered why he chose her. Every time she asked him to do a chore around the house, all Jim heard in his mind was his mother, his father, or both of them ranting at him, calling him names, and making him feel like nothing was good enough.

It wasn't that his wife was like his mother—in fact, she was far from it. It was just the notion of doing household chores that brought these memories to the surface, and Jim incorrectly associated them with his wife. After breaking down in tears after not meeting his wife's expectations for a clean kitchen, she knew there was something wrong. Jim told her about all the abuse and how he couldn't stop hearing his parents' voices, berating him. His wife wisely took him for counseling to help him stop associating his negative self-talk with her.

The first step to confronting NST is to realize that the people we associate with the voices are not the true authors of those thoughts; our minds are. Our thoughts and negative self-talk are triggered by memories of negative events, or events with a negative outcome, and how those around us responded *at the time*. It's a negative nugget burrowed into the deep recesses of our brains, just waiting for the perfect time to jump into the limelight and say, "Aha! See! We told you so!" Negative self-talk seeks to validate what others have said about us all our lives.

Next, we need to realize that NST is a reaction to an event in the present that is similar to something that happened in the past. This is called a trigger. When something in the present reminds us of a past trauma and makes us start thinking negatively, that is a trigger.

David's Story

A young boy named David was in a terrible car accident at age 10. The sights, sounds, smells, and sensations from that event were prominently imprinted in David's memories.

Five years later, during driver's education, David was forced to watch films of car crashes that resulted from teens either driving recklessly or driving drunk. His mind tells him, "See, this is why you shouldn't drive. You know you'll kill someone."

Even though David was not responsible for the accident he was in, hearing the sirens and seeing the crushed cars are enough to bring his negative self-talk to the surface. David doesn't realize he is so afraid of crashing that his mind is using NST to convince him not to get behind the wheel.

What can David do to confront something like this? He has to start by realizing—consciously—that the accident he was in had nothing to do with whether or not he'll be a good driver. In fact, David needs to recognize that the experience of the car crash may make him an even safer, more cautious driver because he knows how dangerous it can be. David's negative self-talk is trying to convince him that he has already failed as a driver, but David must put a stop to that line of thinking.

NST is typically generated by some kind of failure, perceived failure, or apparent shortcoming. People who have been through trauma or have severe anxiety, depression, and mood disorders are particularly susceptible to NST because they see failure all around, in everything they do. Whether through past trauma or altered brain chemistry, they have an incredibly difficult time recognizing success, particularly their own.

You know these types of people, right? They can't take a compliment. They don't like to be the center of attention. They don't think they deserve any type of reward or accolade.

Their ability to feel successful is completely bogged down and drowned out by negative self-talk.

In fact, negative self-talk is so ingrained in the past that it can keep you stagnant. Staying "in the past can represent a kind of self-indulgence. It can interfere with your creating or (in some alternate shape or form) recreating past joys. Ultimately, it's pointless to employ memory to hold onto what may have been lost many, many years ago. And as a result of not letting go of the past, you may rob yourself of present opportunities to reach out for what may still lie within your grasp" (Seltzer, 2011).

Keith's Story

Keith was one of those who couldn't let go of the past. The negative self-talk was so intense that it clouded his judgment about decisions being made in the present. As a child, Keith was beaten by his mother. His father left them when he was only three years old, and his mother blamed him for that. She blamed him anytime something went wrong. It got to the point that Keith had to weigh every decision so carefully, he was paralyzed to act. He couldn't risk making a bad decision that his mother would interpret as stupidity, recklessness, or outright defiance. If he didn't choose properly, there was a beating in his future.

As an adult, Keith still couldn't make decisions. He lost many girlfriends because even though he was an amazing boyfriend (loving, kind, attentive, funny, and cute), he could *never* make a decision. They didn't understand that when it came time to make a choice, all Keith could hear was his mother's voice: "Why would you do that? Are you stupid?" "Who gave you permission to do that?" "Don't you have any common sense?" Decisions made Keith defensive and frightened, so rather than making a choice, he let everyone else choose everything.

Keith would even give up things he wanted—and knew he could have—for fear of making the wrong choice. When his car broke down, he went to a car dealership to browse. As he drove into the lot, he went straight past the new vehicles and directly to the used car lot. His mother's voice reminded him that he "didn't deserve a new car" and that he didn't "make enough money for a new car," neither of which was true.

When Keith mentioned to his doctor that he was having trouble with decision-making, the doctor asked him lots of questions before determining that Keith would benefit from counseling. He needed someone to talk to who wouldn't be a threat—a male counselor. Since the root of his issues stemmed from his mother's abuse, Keith needed a man to talk to who could help him unravel his fear of making choices and learn that he, indeed, has value and worth.

Think for a moment about your day. Did you spend it defending yourself from negative self-talk? Or did you let it rule you? Did you waste hours arguing with yourself? Or did you simply allow the voices to dictate your choices? What did you accomplish by doing so? Were you able to move forward in your life?

More often than not, people bogged down by NST cannot move forward without help. Admitting that something is wrong and that you don't know how to handle it is the first step to confronting the NST. You can't solve a problem unless you acknowledge it. Therapy can help you separate past traumas from your present reality. Through various types of treatment, you can not only bravely and strongly confront NST, but also *defeat it.*

Never, never, never give up!
—Winston Churchill

Part III: Treatment and Recovery Strategies

Remember Darcy? She was afraid people would think she was crazy if she told them about the negative voices. But everyone experiences negative self-talk every once in a while. It is simply part of how the human brain works.

Did you catch that? *Everyone* experiences negative self-talk every once in a while. Even the people who seem to have the most perfect lives will eventually deal with NST.

"According to the National Science Foundation the average person has about 12,000 to 60,000 thoughts per day. Of those, 80% are negative and 95% are exactly the same repetitive thoughts as the day before and about 80% negative. What we tell ourselves on an ongoing basis reflects not only the way we think but how we feel and act. In other words our thoughts influence how we create our reality" (Simone, 2017).

Have you ever made that connection? "Our thoughts influence how we create our reality." Isn't reality objective? Absolutely not! Reality is different for each individual. Our perceptions are completely individualized. Two people in the same room wearing the same clothing and facing the same direction will most definitely have different perceptions of that moment of reality. One person may be focusing on the background noise and voices of others in the room. The other person may be fixated on an object, a color, or the smell of someone's cologne.

Because reality is a subjective concept—yes, concept—it's not a thing. The ability of one person to overcome NST is completely subjective as well. "Most people don't realize it, but as we go about our daily lives we are constantly thinking about and interpreting the situations we find ourselves in. It's as though we have an internal voice inside our head that determines how we perceive every situation. Self-talk is often skewed towards the negative, and sometimes it's just plain wrong" (Martin, 2016).

Think about your reality. What tasks and activities occur in your reality on a daily basis? Could some of those daily activities be feeding NST or triggering it? If you hate looking in the mirror because your negative self-talk is all about how ugly you are, what can you do about it for the moment? Is there a temporary fix until you get NST under control? Of course there is! Take the mirror down. Cover it with a sheet. Get a smaller mirror you only use when flossing or doing your hair. That way, you can focus on the task at hand rather than staring at yourself. Taking the trigger away will help keep the negative self-talk at bay.

What about the people in your life? Sometimes, it's impossible to escape negative self-talk because you can't escape the origins of it.

Justin's Story

Justin grew up with an alcoholic mother and abusive father. Both were supremely selfish and had no use for Justin. In fact, his mother said many times during her drunken stupors that she wished she'd had an abortion. His father resented him because if "that lazy bitch hadn't gotten pregnant, I wouldn't have had to marry her." He blamed Justin for everything that went wrong in his life, and he showed his displeasure with his fists.

Despite this dangerous home life, Justin did well in school—well enough to earn a scholarship to college in another state. He excitedly told his parents about it. He could go to school and they wouldn't have to pay for it. Isn't that great!

His mother just turned and walked out of the room—her wineglass needed to be filled. His father was fuming. "Oh, great! You were born and I couldn't go to college, but *you* get to go. How is that great, boy? Tell me, how is that wonderful news?"

Justin's joy was short-lived. His father insisted he turn down the scholarship, go to the local community college, and pay for it on his own. "I didn't get any free rides, boy, so neither will you!" Since he couldn't go away, Justin had to live at home. Every day after classes, his father told him how lucky he was and that working hard never killed anyone. It would make him strong.

Every day in class, Justin would try to focus, but he'd only hear his father's voice, berating him and demeaning his existence. If Justin got good grades, he had to hide it. Justin's successes only reminded his father of his own failures.

The negative self-talk got so bad that Justin couldn't sleep, couldn't eat, and didn't want to leave his room. He started skipping classes and shifts at work. The negative self-talk beat him down so badly that he developed major depression, but he certainly couldn't tell his parents. It was only through his psychology professor's noticing his depression that Justin got help in time.

And in the case of Justin's family, his father clearly suffered from NST as well. He not only experienced it; he expressed it: "That stupid kid was born so I couldn't go to college." "I had to get married because of that damn baby."

Justin's father allowed those negative thoughts to control his actions. Could he have gone to college with a young wife and baby? Possibly—with a lot of hard work. Did he have to marry the woman he impregnated? Not necessarily, but he felt pressured by his family and hers until he felt like he had no choice. Negative self-talk is a burden for anyone to bear, and it can become a generational passage.

When your negative self-talk gets so bad that you are drinking to drown out the voices or abusing your loved ones to feel some measure of control, it is definitely time to seek treatment.

Chapter 6: Options for Treatment

In order to defeat negative self-talk and find a way to cope with and heal from our negative pasts, there are multiple options. If you suffer from a mental health condition, your doctor can help you determine which option is the best choice for you. Not everyone can thrive in every treatment situation. You have to make the best choice for yourself and your situation. But everything starts by deciding *you want to be healthy*.

There are many things we can do every day "to get into good mental and emotional health. Every day, make sure you meet your needs for safety, love, power, fun, and freedom. Be sure you meet these needs in respectful and responsible ways. Be sure that your relationships are not based on you attempting to control the other person. Instead, work toward managing your differences with other people in a loving, respectful, and mutually satisfying way. Practice connecting habits with all the people in your life:

- Caring
- Listening
- Supporting
- Encouraging
- Respecting
- Befriending
- Trusting
- Accepting

Each one of us can work to improve good emotional and mental health right now!" (Buck, 2013)

When we want to be happy, when we work to be happy, when we choose to be healthy, all of these things come into play. But if you can't do it on your own, there is no shame in searching for alternatives. Millions of people every year benefit from cognitive behavioral therapy, support groups, and even Eastern philosophies like meditation.

Cognitive Behavioral Therapy

One of the primary forms of therapeutic treatment, or modern therapy, is called cognitive behavioral therapy, or CBT. This is the most widely used form of treatment for any patient struggling with mental health issues or who just needs to straighten out the negative self-talk in their life. Most therapists, counselors, psychologists, and psychiatrists will use or are at least familiar with the concepts and principles that drive CBT:

CBT is an approach for which there is ample scientific evidence that the methods that have been developed *actually produce change*. In this manner, CBT differs from many other forms of psychological treatment. CBT is based on several core principles, including:

- Psychological problems are based, in part, on faulty or unhelpful ways of thinking.
- Psychological problems are based, in part, on learned patterns of unhelpful behavior.
- People suffering from psychological problems can learn better ways of coping with them,

thereby relieving their symptoms and becoming more effective in their lives.

CBT treatment usually involves efforts to change thinking patterns:

- Learning to recognize one's distortions in thinking that are creating problems, and then to reevaluate them in light of reality.
- Gaining a better understanding of the behavior and motivation of others.
- Using problem-solving skills to cope with difficult situations.
- Learning to develop a greater sense of confidence is one's own abilities.

CBT treatment also usually involves efforts to *change behavioral patterns*. These strategies might include:

- Facing one's fears instead of avoiding them.
- Using role playing to prepare for potentially problematic interactions with others.
- Learning to calm one's mind and relax one's body. (APA, 2017)

Many people who struggle with negative self-talk are afraid to ask for help. They don't know what "therapy" is or what would happen to them if they went. Some of them may be discouraged by family members who don't want anyone in their family labeled "a crazy person" and who think that therapy is only for people who are nuts.

But a review of the techniques and precepts above tells you one thing: the use of CBT is a time-tested, scientifically based set of principles and actions meant to help the patient heal. If you look at the lists carefully, you will notice that several of the techniques used in CBT are things we've already mentioned in this book.

While these may not be universal tools, the foundations of the concepts have been in place for decades, and there is no reason to fear seeking out a therapist who specializes in cognitive behavioral therapy, especially when your life appears to be fully in order, yet your negative self-talk won't give you a break.

Joann's Story

Joann was a bright, talented legal secretary. She thoroughly enjoyed her work and didn't aspire to anything more. She made enough money to live comfortably, had a great social network of supportive friends, and was engaged to be married to a wonderful man who worked for the city as a civic engineer. A few months after getting engaged, Joann was ready to call it off. She was scared that her fiancé would find out the truth: Joann thought she herself was worthless.

For most of her life, her father had pressured Joann—an only child—to become a great and successful lawyer like him. After her mother passed away during her senior year of high school, Joann lost the only protection she had from her father's demands on her future. The loss of his wife drove Joann's father to start drinking excessively. When he came home drunk, he railed at Joann, telling her how if she didn't become a lawyer, she would be a failure, or if she didn't bring her grades up, she wouldn't get in to law school. He balked at how she never seemed to "keep the house up" like her mother did. He would throw his hands up in frustration and tell Joann he wished it had been her who died.

Every day that Joann walked into the law firm where she happily worked, she could hear her father's voice: "A damned secretary. What a waste. You should be working in that corner office making a million a year." She never let it show, but those words from her father cut her to the core.

Each time Joann turned in a file to her supervising attorney, he would smile, thank her for her excellent work, and have another file waiting for her. Joann would take it, return the smile, thank her boss, and return to her desk. There, her father's voice was waiting: "You know he's only being nice because he wants to sleep with you. He doesn't respect you. You are never going to live up to your potential."

Every day that Joann returned home, she would lay her keys on the kitchen counter, look around her small but very nice apartment, and hear nothing but derision: "Geez, you couldn't even rinse your coffee mug before you went to work? Are you ever going to do laundry? Why is the trash can still full?"

Joann was so terrified of her negative self-talk that she couldn't bear the thought of putting her fiancé into a marriage that would ultimately fail, or so she thought.

Luckily, a good friend noticed Joann's depressed mood and accompanied her to see her family doctor. When the doctor asked Joann about her low mood, Joann burst into tears and said, "I am so sorry I wasted your time. I'm hopeless. There's nothing anyone can do to help a worthless case like me!"

Fortunately, the doctor recognized the signs of depression and immediately set Joann up with a therapist who

63

specialized in CBT. Joann fought going, as she thought it was just one more sign that she was a failure of a human being. But her good friend wouldn't let her get out of it. She drove Joann to therapy and stayed in the waiting room during Joann's evaluation.

The therapist asked Joann about negative self-talk. Joann didn't understand. When the therapist explained what it was, Joann whispered, "It's always my dad." That was her first step to healing through the process of cognitive behavioral therapy. She eventually came up with her own mantra: "It's not my dad saying it; it's my mind replaying it."

Some people who struggle with negative self-talk are actually happy to embrace therapy because they can finally put a name to the devil inside. "An awesome benefit of therapy is that it not only helps you understand yourself better, but it helps you understand other people. When we hold negative thoughts in without processing them, they become ingrained so that we see the world through that lens—and we make lots of assumptions that may or may not be true. Since big and small problems are going to come up from time to time, knowing how to deal with them in a healthy way is an essential skill.

"Have you ever noticed how turning a problem around and around in your head often gets you precisely nowhere? It's so easy to feel dwarfed by a problem when it's just an amorphous blob in your head—but talking about it gives it a beginning, middle, and end. And that helps you wrap your brain around it. Seeing a psychologist can be a huge relief in-and-of itself since you know you're taking action against what ails you. It [is] also comforting just knowing that you have a

built-in support structure that you can go to once a week"
(Walton, 2014).

Carol's Story

Carol knew she had a psychological problem, but she couldn't put her finger on it. Her NST was such a constant presence in her life that she couldn't separate it from her daily stream of consciousness. There was nothing worse than knowing something was wrong and not being able to name it. Did she have depression? Bipolar disorder (it ran in her family)? God, was it schizophrenia?

When you don't know what is wrong, you tend to catastrophize. "Catastrophizing is a cognitive distortion that prompts people to jump to the worst possible conclusion, usually with very limited information or objective reason to despair. When a situation is upsetting, but not necessarily catastrophic, they still feel like they are in the midst of a crisis" (Psychology, 2021). This is where Carol found herself—in the midst of crisis after crisis that only she could recognize as crises.

"This pattern of thinking can itself be destructive because unnecessary and persistent worry (brought on by negative self-talk) can lead to heightened anxiety and depression. But through learning to identify and reframe initially exaggerated conclusions, along with other techniques, people with a tendency to make a proverbial mountain out of a molehill can get a better hold on their negative thoughts" (Psychology, 2021).

During her annual physical, Carol told her family doctor about the constant state of crisis management she seemed to live in. After some pointed questions, the doctor advised Carol to see a therapist to identify how and why her negative self-talk was leading her to catastrophize. "Negative self-talk? What is that?" Carol asked. Once the doctor explained it, Carol uttered a huge sigh of relief. Now she had a name for the devilish driver of her constant crisis control. Carol couldn't wait to embrace therapy full on.

Once Carol knew there was help for her problem, she couldn't get on the therapy train fast enough. Even though her grandmother, who grew up a tough farm kid in the Great Depression, thought she was weak to seek therapy, Carol shoved grandma's concerns aside and decided it was time for her to start living instead of reacting.

Cognitive behavioral therapy isn't for everyone. If your family physician or loved ones seem to notice you aren't behaving like yourself, listen to them, but decide for yourself what treatment option is best for you. If you are a deeply spiritual person, or if you just prefer to have someone to talk to who understands your problem, there might be a recovery program just waiting for you to fall into its arms of peace and acceptance.

Recovery Programs

Alcoholics have AA; narcotic addicts have NA. What program is out there for someone with unrelenting NST? Believe it or not, there are multiple programs you can investigate that could be your key to beating back negative self-talk.

If you're a Christian, and even if you're not, Celebrate Recovery might be a great option for you. This Christ-centered recovery program is based on the 12 steps proven to be successful in AA and NA and their eight principles taken from the Beatitudes, a list of attributes and behaviors Christ gave to His followers:

> Jesus laid out these principles for happiness in the Sermon on the Mount in the gospel of Matthew, chapter 5. Today we call them "the Beatitudes." Change, Jesus says, can be ours, but the pathway to change and happiness may not be exactly what we're expecting. From a conventional viewpoint, most of the following eight statements don't make sense. At first they even sound like contradictions. But when you fully understand what Jesus is saying, you'll realize these eight statements are God's pathway to wholeness, growth, and spiritual maturity.
>
> "Happy are those who know they are spiritually poor."
> "Happy are those who mourn, for they shall be comforted."
> "Happy are the meek." "Happy are the pure in heart."
> "Happy are those whose greatest desire is to do what God requires."
> "Happy are those who are merciful."
> "Happy are those who work for peace."
> "Happy are those who are persecuted because they do what God requires." (Baker, 1991)

The greatest part of Celebrate Recovery is the pure, unquestioning acceptance the minute you walk through the door. For someone who constantly battles negative self-talk, that kind of judgment-free acceptance is something strange and new.

Each meeting begins with a time of fellowship, just meeting people and getting to know them. When the meeting starts, you will hear and sing songs of worship that can uplift you and fill your spirit. If you've never been to church before or even thought about religion, that's okay! CR is based on Christian principles, but you don't have to be a Christian to get something out of it. After singing, the group meeting is held, where you either hear a testimony from someone in recovery, or a lesson based on one of the 12 steps or eight principles. Everything here is meant to help you face your negativity and focus on the positives you can find when you leave NST and other hurts behind.

If you are a Buddhist, or have an interest in learning about Buddhism, you can try Recovery Dharma. Their goal is to use Buddhist practices and principles to heal. Their primary focus is on addiction, and that word itself has many meanings. Addicts can be drawn to alcohol, drugs, food, sex, codependence, and, yes, self-talk. Just as in Celebrate Recovery, you don't have to be a believer to attend Recovery Dharma:

> Our weekly meetings are a chance to come together to support recovery through the practice of meditation, study of the Dharma, listening to each other, and building community.

> A typical meeting starts with a few short explanatory readings, then a guided meditation. Meetings will then typically do a shared reading to foster discussion, or a speaker may talk about a topic of their choice. There

is also an opportunity for members of the group to share. Each meeting is free to choose the format that works best for them. (Recovery, 2020)

Recovery Dharma also invites anyone who is looking to heal from any negative behavior, whether it's caused by substance use, codependency, gambling, eating disorders, relationships, technology, or any obsessive or habitual pattern that creates suffering. "We've found that this Buddhist-inspired path can lead to liberation from the suffering of addiction, and we support you in finding your own path to recovery" (Recovery, 2020).

And it's good to know you don't have to choose a religious-based recovery program; you can choose SMART Recovery. Self-Management and Recovery Training (SMART) is a global community of mutual-support groups:

> If you want to address any addiction or harmful habit, SMART Recovery can help. Major changes can be overwhelming. SMART's practical tools and social supports are proven effective to support and sustain successful long-term life change. Harmful habits include substance addictions (to alcohol and other drugs), as well as activity addictions (to behaviors like sex, relationships, spending, gambling, eating, exercise, and self-injury). No matter your harmful habit, SMART can help you change it.

> SMART is not just any mutual-support program. Our science-based approach emphasizes self-empowerment and self-reliance . . . You choose how to personalize your own plan for successful change.

SMART can be used both as a stand-alone program or in combination with other recovery paths. SMART Recovery recognizes the only one who can become truly expert on your recovery is you. (SMART, 2021)

And this is just the tip of the recovery iceberg! There are hundreds of programs out there ready to help you turn your back on your negative self-talk and start living the life *you* want to live. And sometimes, it's the support and insistence of a really good friend that gets you into a recovery program you can succeed in.

Sara's Story

Sara had a real problem with negative self-talk. The worst part was she knew it. She knew exactly what the problem was, but her husband was so against psychotherapy that she didn't dare go. Then a friend told her about Celebrate Recovery. Sara wasn't interested in being dragged into a Bible-thumping revival. Her friend Michelle laughed and said to her, "I promise—no Bible-thumping, no tent revivals! Just people who are broken and want to help each other heal."

It took a couple of weeks of convincing, but Michelle finally got Sara to come to a meeting. Everyone Sara met was kind, compassionate, and genuinely happy to meet her. Sara was amazed at how open everyone was about their problems and how they extended brotherly love to one another without judgment. And after the worship, Sara was amazed to hear a testimony from a woman who suffered from food addiction and who had allowed negative self-talk to sabotage her efforts at healthy eating. The woman said, "Every time I would show weight loss on the scale, that little voice in the back of my head would say, 'Maybe, but you *know* you're gonna gain it back.'"

Sara was able to find people to talk to who truly understood what she was going through. She was amazed at the place she found it, but just knowing that there were people out there who wanted to help her and cared about her recovery gave her the motivation to start confronting her negative self-talk.

This and many programs like it are saving people from their pain and leading them to healing every single day. "Maximize the amount of time that you spend with people you enjoy being around. Connecting with others who radiate positivity and have similar interests will excite and energize you. On the flip side, people you don't relate to or who have negative outlooks, complain often, or make poor choices will only drain your energy. Be selective in the company you keep. Maintaining a compassionate mindset is another way to improve your mental health. One example of practicing this way of thinking is called kind attention. For example, try to make eye contact with a stranger and smile, while thinking 'I wish you well.' This positive act can, instead, keep you from judging that person. Judging others can cause us to place judgment on ourselves, and that type of negative internal dialogue can be exhausting" (Mayo, 2020). Yet, there are still other ways to approach reducing your negative self-talk.

Biofeedback and Neurofeedback

Biofeedback is what some people would call an "old school" therapeutic technique. By definition, biofeedback is "a type of therapy that uses sensors attached to your body to measure key body functions. Biofeedback is intended to help you learn more about how your body works. This information may help you to develop better control over certain body functions and address health concerns" (Kranz, 2017).

While biofeedback is generally used to identify physical health issues, there is real value in using neurofeedback to understand how your mind works. When you have to deal with chronic stress, that stress can create dramatic effects in your overall health, including high blood pressure, high body temperature, and a disruption of proper brain function.

"By promoting a more effective mental and physical response to stress, biofeedback aims to help you control body processes like your heart rate and blood pressure. These body processes were once thought to be completely involuntary" (Kranz, 2017).

So if biofeedback can help teach us how to control our blood pressure and heart rate, why can't neurofeedback help us stop negative self-talk? ". . . neurofeedback allows a person to gain mastery over anxiety, focus, concentration, and relaxation. It also creates flexibility in the mind. Cognitive flexibility is as important as physical flexibility . . . [and] neurofeedback is Physical Therapy for the brain." Doctors and scientists can use "qEEG (quantitative electroencephalogram) and EEG biofeedback (also called neurofeedback or neurotherapy) to train individuals to alter their brainwaves" (Neuroagility, 2021).

Before moving on, it is essential to understand that neurofeedback cannot be successful without the processes of neuroplasticity. Neuroplasticity "can be defined as the ability of the nervous system to respond to intrinsic or extrinsic stimuli by reorganizing its structure, function and connections" (Cramer et al., 2011). Neuroplasticity is the foundation for the success of neurofeedback. If the brain did not have the ability to reorganize structures and connections, neurofeedback would not be possible.

And it is the neuroplasticity of the mind that even allows us to consider the possibility of rewiring our brains to expel negative self-talk. A study on neuroplasticity of the brain from 2016 suggests that "the focus of this review is on driving neuroplasticity in a positive direction using evidence-based interventions that also have the potential to improve general health. One goal is to provide an overview of the many ways new neuroscience can inform treatment protocols to empower and motivate clients to make the lifestyle choices that could help build brain power and could increase adherence to healthy lifestyle changes that have also been associated with simultaneously enhancing vigorous longevity, health, happiness, and wellness" (Shaffer, 2016).

If we can increase our brain power through neuroplasticity and neurofeedback, we have a much better chance of rewiring our brains not only to get rid of negative self-talk but also to ensure a longer, happier, and healthier life. As scientists continue to pursue studies on a person's ability to control the development of their brains, we come closer to our next step in evolution.

But along with the scientific, there are other practices and techniques that can be successfully integrated in the rewiring of the brain. The primary method is meditation.

One of the key processes that exist to help us with a true mind-body connection is meditation. "Meditation is considered as a type of mind-body complementary medicine. It can give a sense of calmness, peace and balance that benefits both emotional well-being and overall health" (Ramesh et al., 2013). This practice has been used to train the mind to focus attention and emotion for hundreds of years.

In the past decade or two, researchers and practitioners have expressed increased interest in the "neural basis of meditative practices," as empirical evidence is continuing to grow supporting the hypothesis that meditation can lead to significant improvement in both cognitive function and alterations in the structure of the brain (Fox et al., 2016). Using meditation as a way to control your thoughts—and therefore, NST —is not a new consideration in the scientific community. During an overview of the most recent studies on meditation and brain activity, Fox et al. (2016) determined that compassionate meditation (where you focus on loving yourself, loving others, and altruism) can lead to changes in brain activity and positive, meaningful changes in behavior.

While meditation does continue to have a reputation for being a strange way to focus, science is learning more and more every day about how powerful our brains are and how we can take control of negative self-talk.

Is there just one way to meditate? Heavens, no! Is there a book out there to help you find a way to meditate? There are millions! So how do you know what path or process to follow to use meditation in rewiring your brain?

Thankfully, we can break that down for you here. First, it is important to understand the basic definitions and principles of meditation. Meditation itself is a practice where an individual uses a technique—for example, mindfulness, focusing on a single thought, or focusing on a particular object—to train attention and awareness and achieve a mentally clear and emotionally calm and stable state. The initial purpose is to reach a state where you are hyperaware of your mind-body connection. This cannot be done in the first session.

Practicing meditation can be time-consuming. Some people, particularly those who are most open to the experience, can achieve a level of mind-body awareness with just a bit of practice. Others, particularly those who have been bogged down by negativity or are not open to the concepts of meditation (mindfulness, transcendentalism, and ascension), will have a harder time finding that moment of mind-body connection. This connection is central to the practice of meditation and absolutely vital to attain if you have any hope of rewiring your brain.

For the beginner, there are some steps that you should follow to get into a good routine to practice meditation. It is important to engage in meditation regularly, starting with 20-minute sessions that gradually increase to one hour (Bobby, 2020):

Set aside a special place
Whether it is outdoors or indoors, choose a place with a pleasant atmosphere that is free of distractions. An uncluttered area decorated with items that calm the senses, such as incense, bamboo, mandalas, or mild scented oils, can help make the place sacred and unique.

Because the state of meditation exudes powerful vibrations, repeated practice in this space will eventually fill it with the right energy.

Choose a time
Meditation can be done anytime and anywhere, but it is important to choose a time when the mind is free of everyday concerns and there are no disturbances. The ideal time for regular practice is during the precious hour of dawn or dusk, when the atmosphere is flooded with soothing light and abundant with serene spiritual energy.

Use the same time and place each day
Just as the body becomes accustomed to sleeping or eating at specific times, meditating at the same place and time each day trains the body and mind to switch off and respond to stillness comfortably and quickly. Once the practice becomes a habit, you'll find yourself seeking meditation instinctively.

Sit with the back, neck, and head in a straight line
Be seated in a steady and upright, yet relaxed position, ensuring that there is no tension in stress areas such as the forehead, jaw, or shoulders. The line of the spine, neck, and head should be lengthened, tall, and straight. Facing the North or East attracts the Earth's most positive magnetic vibrations—grab on to that positive energy of the universe.

Instruct the mind to remain quiet
Consciously establishing discipline of the mind right at the beginning provides a clean slate in preparation for the

meditation session. Avoid being overly concerned with what is currently happening, reminiscing about past events, or dwelling upon what is going to take place in the future.

Regulate your breathing
Start with approximately five minutes of deep and conscious abdominal breathing that brings fresh oxygen to the brain and aids in concentration. Then begin to slow the breathing down.

Establish a rhythmic breathing pattern
Continue repetitions of inhaling for three seconds and exhaling for three seconds. This pattern of rhythmic breathing controls the flow of prana, or vital energy, and helps to still the mind.

For your first few sessions, let your mind wander
Trying to force the mind to focus will only make it more restless and create more thoughts. Being patient and loving with yourself, on the other hand, means knowing without a doubt that the mind will eventually settle into a place of stillness.

When you are comfortable with the process, bring your mind to rest on a focal point
Focus upon either the Ajna Chakra, the point between the eyebrows (also known as your Third Eye); or the Anahata Chakra, in the region of the heart. You want to focus on these areas as the heart is the center of the body and the Third Eye is the center of the mind. The study of Chakras is another technique to help you strengthen the

mind-body connection and will be discussed after meditation.

Meditate

While still conscious of your focal point, allow the vibrations of focused thought or repetitions of sound created by this constant state of focus to lead to pure thought. This is meditation. In that state of pure thought, focus on emptying the garbage that feeds and fuels negative self-talk.

When you are able to reach a state of meditation on a regular basis, it can help you start eliminating negative self-talk and reduce your stress and anxiety. The practice of identifying and clearing your chakras (an Eastern holistic practice) can also help increase and improve your mind-body connection.

The use and study of chakras has grown along with the popularity of yoga and New Age philosophies. "They are a complex and ancient energy system that originated in India. They were first mentioned in the Vedas, ancient sacred texts of spiritual knowledge dating from 1500 to 1000 BC. Chakra (cakra in Sanskrit) means 'wheel' and refers to energy points in your body. They are thought to be spinning disks of energy that should stay 'open' and aligned, as they correspond to bundles of nerves, major organs, and areas of our energetic body that affect our emotional and physical well-being" (Stelter, 2016).

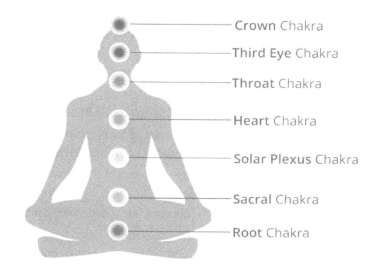

Crown Chakra
Third Eye Chakra
Throat Chakra
Heart Chakra
Solar Plexus Chakra
Sacral Chakra
Root Chakra

For our purposes here, we will focus on the crown chakra and heart chakra. "The crown chakra is linked to every other chakra (and therefore every organ in this system), and so it affects not just all of those organs, but also our brain and nervous system. It is considered the chakra of enlightenment and represents our connection to our life's purpose and spirituality. The heart chakra is the middle of the seven chakras, so it bridges the gap between our upper and lower chakras, and it also represents our ability to love and connect to others. When out of alignment, it can make us feel lonely, insecure, and isolated" (Stelter, 2016).

So how do we combine meditation and chakra practices to help us with negative self-talk? Well, once you have reached a place where you can meditate with regularity, you can then start clearing your chakras during meditation.

"The crown chakra connects you to the wider universal energy, so when this area has a block, isolation or emotional distress can occur. This may present as an inability to set or follow through on goals or an overall lack of direction and feelings of disconnection" (Lechner, 2019). If your crown chakra is blocked by negative self-talk, you will definitely experience emotional distress.

Next, you should focus on clearing your heart chakra. "The heart chakra is associated with air, so breathing deeply will help to clear the energy at this level" (Lechner, 2019). How many times have you been so bogged down by NST that you feel suffocated? Clearing your heart chakra will open up your ability to breathe deeply and clear out any negative energy created by the negative self-talk.

So how do we clear our chakras? Clearing our "chakras refers to the idea that when all of our chakras are open, energy can run through them freely, and harmony exists between the physical body, mind, and spirit. The key to opening the crown chakra is one simple question: 'How can I best serve the whole?' If there is anywhere in your life (meditation, journaling, coaching, conversation) where you are asking about your purpose, change the question from 'What is my purpose?' to 'How can I best serve the whole?' Meditate on this question and write down whatever thoughts arise. Simply asking this question activates the crown chakra" (Cameron, 2020).

When we begin to clear the heart chakra, we focus on love for ourselves and others:

Close your eyes and visualize yourself sitting in front of you. Wish yourself the following:

80

May I feel safe.
May I be healthy.
May I be joyful.
May I know love.

Next, visualize someone in your life whom you love or appreciate. Wish them the same phrases of loving-kindness:

May he/she feel safe.
May he/she be healthy.
May he/she be joyful.
May he/she know love.

Next, visualize someone in your life whom you have conflict with or someone whom you find challenging. Wish them the same:

May he/she feel safe.
May he/she be healthy.
May he/she be joyful.
May he/she know love.

Sit in meditation for five minutes, bathing in the feelings you have generated for yourself and others. (Cameron, 2020)

By focusing on love for yourself and others, there is no room for negative self-talk to get a grip on you. NST is the opposite of love, so having a clear heart and a clear mind (crown) that are fully focused on love and the positive energy of the universe will, if nothing else, drown out the negative self-talk. The practices here are just the beginning to the next big step in getting rid of negative self-talk.

If you can change your mind, you can change your life.
—William James

Part IV: Looking Within

If you've sought treatment, that's fantastic! It's a sign of courage and strength to say, "I need help." Hopefully, your treatment includes not only psychological components but also practices in defining your "self." If you've joined a recovery group and found a new, stronger support system, that's amazing! Take advantage of that new support system to help you when times get tough and your NST is out of control. If you've started your meditation practices and started identifying the power of your chakras, that's awesome! Look forward to finding your inner peace and the balance and harmony NST is stealing from your life.

Meditation and chakra cleansing are just two practices that can help you emotionally and spiritually. Our crown chakra is a connection to the wider universe, and there is science to back up the existence of energy within us that connects to the world outside of us.

Chapter 7: The Energy of the Mind

You may think that "finding yourself" is just a cliché, but nothing could be further from the truth. There are experts and inspirational people who have proven that you have the power to search your mind and identify who you are at your core. This can be done through various avenues in meditation, prayer, or other spiritual practices. But to be successful, you must be open to new ideas and concepts that could directly contradict your personal spiritual beliefs.

No one is saying you should turn your back on your beliefs. All that is required is that you are willing to agree that there are a vast number of things in the universe that we simply can't see or don't yet understand. There is nothing wrong with being a Christian who firmly believes in prayer and who also uses meditation to deal with stress. There is nothing wrong with being a Buddhist who believes in the Universal Truths and the Chosen Path and who also prays or chants as a way to calm the heart and mind.

Consciousness is defined as "the fact of awareness by the mind of itself and the world." Your mind has an awareness of itself and the world around it. Does that mean your brain is its own sentient being? Yes and no. We are in charge of the body in the sense that we make decisions about our actions, we react to stimuli, we learn new things, we feel pain, and we experience feelings. But our brains, at the unconscious level, perceive thousands of stimuli in the world around us without our being aware of them. Perhaps, without us knowing, our brains perceive different levels of the universe that we don't know—yet. That is both exciting and frightening at the same time.

So how do we use this understanding to help us stop negative self-talk? By learning to be more aware of our own mind and spirit as well as the world around us. We start by believing in all three—our minds and the world are concrete, but our spirit is an abstract concept. Is there science that proves each one of us carries a spirit? Can we feel it or find it? How do we connect the spirit to the mind and the world?

We can begin by examining the most basic elements of our constitution: atoms.

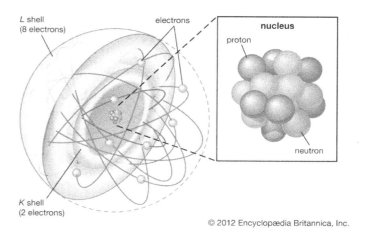

© 2012 Encyclopædia Britannica, Inc.

Basic physics tells us that electrons have a negative charge, protons have a positive charge, and neutrons carry no charge. While this seems simple—and in some ways it is—it is hard to connect that with meditation, chakras, and prayer, don't you think?

It's not as far out as you'd think. What we know about atoms proves that the universe (the world outside the brain) consists of both positive and negative energy, which are balanced by neutral forces. Our bodies are made up of atoms that create our brain, organs, blood, etc., and they function based on whether they are positively or negatively charged. Within our brains, the neurotransmitters that share information do so based on whether they are excited (positively charged) or inhibited (negatively charged).

Atoms are the basic building blocks for the positive and negative energy we experience on a daily basis! Think about the air we breathe. It is also made up of atoms based on the elements in our natural world: oxygen, nitrogen, hydrogen, carbon dioxide, and more. When the air is polluted, there is no longer the perfect balance in the elements we need to function. Our breathing can become affected, or we may become very ill. The same is true for the environment in your brain. When things are out of balance, your brain becomes ill. Negative self-talk is nothing but negative energy that your brain is carrying too much of.

In order to reduce or eliminate your NST, you must be conscious of these two energies and focus your attention on the positive rather than the negative. The more you are in touch with the energies in your mind, the closer you are to gaining control over NST. Sigmund Freud knew, intuitively, that self-knowledge was one of the keys to good mental health.

Chapter 8: Them's Freudin' Words

Of the many scientists and practitioners of psychology, none is more famous than Sigmund Freud. While many of his theories and posits are questionable, there were numerous ideas he put forth that could help us in fighting negative self-talk. Sigmund Freud was certain that self-talk was part of the way we deal with deeper, hidden, stashed-away memories and emotions:

> Freud . . . urged us to be engaged in the pursuit of *self-knowledge*. Here Freud's concerns are familiar: the recovery of painful memories suppressed, the recognition of motives buried, the unearthing of deep emotional conflict, the stripping away of layers of in-capacitating self-deceptions. (Szabados, 1982)

Given the time period Freud lived in (1856–1939), these were amazing, almost laughable statements. No one knew much about the human brain in Freud's time. The term self-talk had not even been invented yet. But his hypothesis seems to have borne itself out over time. Now, 120 years later, the exploration of memories, emotional conflict, and self-deception are a major focus of modern therapy. Freud said the following:

> Our therapy does its work by transforming something unconscious into something conscious, and only succeeds in its work insofar as it is able to effect this transformation. According to the conclusions we have reached so far, neurosis would be the result of a kind

of ignorance, a not knowing of mental processes which should be known. (Szabados, 1982)

Isn't it amazing the insights Freud had? Now, some would argue that Freud was a lunatic, and maybe there is some truth to the notion that he himself was unstable. But that doesn't change the facts. Modern therapy consists of digging around in the unconscious to bring out the emotions that the conscious mind needs to recognize and process. In order to "effect this transformation," we have to be willing to face the memories, conflicts, and self-deceptions head on.

"Freud believed that if you have a strong sense of self, you're capable of understanding your own needs and also intuiting the limits that society puts on you. If you have a strong sense of self, you can move freely through life" (Exploring, 2020). When Freud talked about the limits that society puts on you, doesn't that sound like some of the negative self-talk we might experience? Think about that for a minute: if your negative self-talk includes a teacher or coach who treated you poorly and always brought you down, that is a limitation placed by society. It will take a stronger sense of self for you to defeat those limitations and eliminate those NST voices.

Let's consider the term Freud used: *self-deceptions.* Doesn't that sound an awful lot like negative self-talk? Isn't that exactly what negative self-talk does? It tricks us into thinking something that isn't true, is true.

Interestingly, 120 years ago, Freud recognized that there are distinct parts of our minds that have their own uses and responsibilities: There are two opposing forces that coexist inside of you. On one hand, there is the id, with its basic and elemental needs. On the other hand, you have the superego that reflects the internalization of society's strict rules. The superego limits your desires, aspirations, and dreams.

According to Freud, the id always needs something and always feels unsatisfied in some way. The id is anxious, restless, and doesn't understand the past or the future.

The superego, on the other hand, is a complex entity that makes us hold things back. It limits our freedom, controls our behavior, and crushes our dreams. The superego is a social and cultural entity that shapes us and represses the id.

The ego, the sense of self, is in the middle of all of this. You can't always fulfill your needs with the obligations, dreams, and desires that fit into society's mold. That might be part of the reason why we often don't want to develop a strong sense of self. What's more, sometimes we feel fragmented and lost because of it. (Exploring, 2020)

In 2021, we can understand that our brains have competing needs. Freud's identification of the id, superego, and ego can be described, for our purposes, as the primal needs (id), negative self-talk (superego), and daily thought processes (ego). Freud even expressed what we are trying to achieve here in terms of mental balance: "For these two energies to get along, you have to shine a light on anything you have repressed or hidden inside you. While you work on this aspect of yourself, your hidden needs, motivations, and anxieties will come out" (Exploring, 2020).

Freud may have been considered a quack in his time, but his insights are incredibly useful for the understanding of our consciousness and how we can put our energies in the right place to defeat negative self-talk. We can use his insights to find the voice inside ourselves that is most useful against NST.

Being entirely honest with oneself is a good exercise.
—Sigmund Freud

Chapter 9: Find Your Powerful Voice

We've learned so much so far about how to recognize negative self-talk, how it is defined, and what experts say about it. Now it's time for you to start working on it. It's time to stop listening to the little voice and start talking back—*loudly*!

Within each of us is the power to overcome. Whether or not we do overcome is a choice. That's right; I said it's a choice. But you may be thinking, "I can't overcome a deadly cancer." No, your *body* can't overcome it, but your mind can! If anyone proved this, it was Patrick Swayze.

When the American actor was diagnosed with pancreatic cancer—what some consider to be the deadliest and fastest moving cancer—he could have given up and died. But he sought treatment in hopes of gaining more time to live. He said, "That's one thing I'm not gonna do, is chase, is chase staying alive. I'm not, you know, you'll spend so much time chasing staying alive you won't live, you know? I wanna live" (Brownstein, 2009).

So ask yourself: Do you want to sit back and let negative self-talk consume you like a cancer? Or do you want to live? Say it with me: I wanna live. Say it loud: I WANNA LIVE! Say it like you are tearing the words from your guts:

I WANNA LIVE!

What do you say to your negative self-talk?

I WANNA LIVE!

What do you say to that "little voice" when it is berating you and beating you down?

I WANNA LIVE!

Find that power! Use that powerful voice! You have it! Every human being has a powerful voice that can drown out sorrow, pain, agony, anger, frustration, hurt, and any other negative emotion the cruel world can bring down on us. When you find that power, your "little voice" with its negative self-talk will cower in the deepest corner of your mind, hands over its ears, begging you to stop because it's dying.

Shout at it: **YOU'VE BEEN KILLING ME! IT'S YOUR TURN!** Make sure it knows that now that you have found your power, NST will *never* rule your life again!

Beyond taking charge with your inner voice, there are also strategies you can use to make a positive difference in your self-talk. "You can test, challenge, and change your self-talk. You can change some of the negative aspects of your thinking by challenging the irrational parts and replacing them with more reasonable thoughts. With practice, you can learn to notice your own negative self-talk as it happens, and consciously choose to think about the situation in a more realistic and helpful way" (Martin, 2016).

Thinking about your self-talk in "a more realistic and helpful way" relies on your ability to recognize your reality. Sometimes, our realities are far from what others see, and often they are skewed by our NST. "A good way to test the accuracy of your perceptions might be to ask yourself some challenging question[s]. These questions will help you to check out your self-talk to see whether your current view is reasonable. This will also help you discover other ways of thinking about your situation.

Reality testing
What is my evidence for and against my thinking?
Are my thoughts factual, or are they just my interpretations?
Am I jumping to negative conclusions?
How can I find out if my thoughts are actually true?

Alternative explanations
Are there any other ways that I could look at this situation?
What else could this mean?
If I were being positive, how would I perceive this situation?

Getting perspective
Is this situation as bad as I am making [it] out to be?
What is the worst thing that could happen? How likely is it?
What is the best thing that could happen?
What is most likely to happen?
Is there anything good about this situation? (Martin, 2016)

Asking yourself these questions is a great start to taking back your power. When we are in the grips of NST, we can find it difficult—if not impossible—to connect with our reality. We get hyper-focused on the negativity we are experiencing and the pain it brings. By stepping back and

93

asking yourself these questions, you offer yourself the opportunity to find a way out of the cycle of NST and bring yourself back to a calmer, more reasoned state.

As you work with a therapist, talk with a group, or meditate alone, use the positive energy that you find there to help fuel your inner voice. In fact, why don't you introduce your inner voice process to others? Everyone in the world deals with negative self-talk in one way or another. Why not teach them what you have learned about taking back your power?

At some point, almost everyone has given someone else power over the way they think, feel, or behave. Giving away your personal power robs you of mental strength. But maintaining control in your life requires that you make a conscious choice to take back your power. Before you can create positive change, you need to recognize the ways in which you give your power away:

1. Don't waste energy complaining.

There's a big difference between complaining and problem-solving. Venting to your friends, family, and co-workers keeps you focused on the problem and prevents you from creating a solution. Grumbling implies that you have no power over your situation, and also shows that you lack power over your attitude.

2. Accept responsibility for how you feel.

94

Don't let other people's behavior dictate your emotions. Saying your mother-in-law makes you feel bad about yourself, or claiming that your boss makes you mad, suggests that they have power over how you feel. Instead, accept that it is up to you to manage your emotions, regardless of how others behave.

3. Establish healthy boundaries.

Giving in to guilt trips, or refusing to speak up for yourself, gives power to other people. Rather than blame them for wasting your time or "forcing" you to do something, recognize that you're in charge of yourself. Establish healthy physical and emotional boundaries that give you control over how you spend your time and with whom you spend it.

4. Practice forgiveness.

Holding a grudge against someone who has hurt you doesn't punish the other person—it only punishes you. When you waste valuable time thinking about a person you feel has wronged you, it takes away your ability to enjoy the moment.

Forgiving someone is the best way to take back your power. But to be clear, forgiveness isn't about saying what the person did was OK. It's about choosing to let go of the hurt and anger that interferes with your ability to enjoy life.

5. Know your values.

When you're not clear what your values are, you're at risk of becoming a helpless passenger rather than a confident driver of [your] own life. You'll be at risk of jumping on board with other people's ideas and may be easily led astray. Take back your power by acknowledging your values and living true to what's important to you.

6. Don't waste time on unproductive thoughts.

Have you ever come home from work and spent the entire evening wishing you didn't have to go back again tomorrow? Suddenly, you're giving your eight-hour workday 12 hours of your time. Take control over the thoughts that occupy your mind, so you don't give more brainpower to areas of your life that don't deserve it.

7. Avoid language that implies you're a victim.

Saying things like, "I have to work 60 hours a week," or, "I had no choice but to say yes," infers that you're a victim of unfortunate circumstances. While there will certainly be consequences for the decisions you make, acknowledge that you always have choices.

8. Make your self-worth independent of other people's opinions.

If your self-worth depends on others holding you in high regard, you'll likely become a people-pleaser. Not everyone needs to like you, nor do they have to agree with your lifestyle. Evaluate the merit of criticism you receive, but never allow any one person's opinion determine your self-worth.

9. Be willing to stand out from the crowd.

Self-doubt and fear can lead you to want to blend in with those around you. But trying to fit in with the crowd will cause you to disguise who you really are. Trust that you're mentally strong enough to stand out and dare to be different. (Morin, 2016)

Once you have cleared your mind, harnessed the positive energy of the universe, and taken your power back, you can once again use your powerful voice to tell NST what you are going to do for yourself and your future:

I'M GONNA LIVE!

Part V: Rewire Your Brain

Science suggests that "one of the coolest things about therapy is that it can bring about change at the level of the brain. We think of medication as changing the depressed brain, but there's very compelling evidence that talk therapy does the same. With brain imaging methods, psychotherapy has been shown to alter activity in the medial prefrontal cortex, the anterior cingulate cortex, the hippocampus, and the amygdala. These areas are involved in self-referential thoughts ("me"-centered worry thoughts), executive control, emotion, and fear. One very effective method, cognitive behavior therapy (CBT), helps people identify the negative thought patterns they fall back on habitually—which are no doubt wired into the brain like deep ruts—and replace them with new and more positive mental habits. In addition to helping people experience fewer symptoms of depression and anxiety, it, too, seems to bring about brain changes that are measurable" (Walton, 2014).

Now it's time to fully integrate what you've learned here and start the rewiring process to eliminate negative self-talk. Remember, even though your brain can form thoughts without your permission, it's up to *you* to decide whether to listen and believe or rebel and keep control of your power.

Chapter 10: Be Self-Empowered

Self-empowerment might seem like a ubiquitous, trite expression that has lost its influence through overuse in society. However, there is real truth in the prospect of self-empowerment when it comes to getting control over negative self-talk. One of the first things negative self-talk takes from you is your power.

We all like to believe that we are in control of our lives, though most of us can admit that the majority of our lives are out of control. We live in a chaotic world that is filled with negativity. That can wear anyone down. Remember when we talked about the positive and negative energy in the universe? The amount of negative energy out there right now is tremendous, and we are inundated by it through various means.

If you want to become self-empowered, you must start by cutting off the negative energy in your life. That can mean getting rid of some of your social media accounts, reducing the amount of time you spend watching the news, finding a new job, and even ending toxic relationships that don't provide any positive energy in your life. Negative energy is a vampire—it sucks your energy away and doesn't provide anything in return. It is the primary culprit of your loss of empowerment.

During the feminist movement of the '60s and '70s, one of the key slogans women shouted repeatedly was "Take back your power!" While that may seem like a cliché now, it really isn't. Start your victory over negative self-talk by taking back your power!

Think of the positive energy available to you as your power. Positive energy manifests itself in many ways: love, kindness, generosity, selflessness, and more. The more positive energy you send out into the world, the more there is for everyone to draw from. The more there is to draw from, the more you can increase your empowerment. You can begin regaining your power by loving yourself.

Lucy's Story

Lucy grew up in a cauldron of hatred. Her parents fought constantly—and violently—while she and her siblings hid in terror. They all knew that if they got within arm's length of the battle, they ran the risk of getting hit. As the children grew older, they began to turn on each other. Lucy was the only girl and had four brothers, so she was an easy target. Rather than feeling the instinctive need to protect their baby sister, they each took turns berating her, beating her, and badgering her to no end.

By the time she was 11, Lucy had become stoic and standoffish. She had never known love at home, and the environment in her school was no better. Lucy often showed up to school in dirty clothes, with her hair in knots, without a lunch, and with her homework not done. Her classmates made fun of her "low-class" family, telling her how much she stank of body odor, and how stupid she was that she couldn't finish her homework.

The teachers were overworked, with an average of 30 children per room, and barely had enough time to take attendance after settling the unruly children down and breaking up the inevitable fights that occurred every single day. Most taught the best they could, but there were those who had simply given up.

Lucy could see their hopelessness and felt the same way in her heart. Her brain constantly reminded her, "You're no good." "You're so damned pitiful and stupid." "You'd be better off dead." Her negative self-talk stemmed from the abuse of her brothers and parents. Once, Lucy got too close to one of her parents' battles and got a black eye for her trouble. Numb to her environment, she simply walked into the kitchen to get some ice and put it on her eye. Lucy was so love deprived she couldn't even cry for herself.

The next day, her teacher noticed the black eye. She had been watching Lucy and knew home was not a good environment. She took Lucy to the nurse's office to get checked out. On the walk down the hall, the teacher asked, "Lucy, what happened?"

Lucy replied bluntly, "Got too close to my parents' fight is all." Lucy's flat tone worried her teacher considerably. As the nurse tended to Lucy's eye, her teacher was with the school's guidance counselor making a plan.

Child protective services came to get Lucy after school. Lucy went with them without complaint or fuss. After a thorough shower at the children's shelter, Lucy got new clothes for the first time in years, along with a new hairbrush, toothbrush, and socks. The therapist worked with Lucy for just an hour before realizing that Lucy didn't know how to love—herself or anyone else. She asked Lucy to write down what thoughts she heard in her own head, and Lucy's writings were frightening. Her NST had progressed to self-hatred, the hatred of others, and suicidal ideation.

Within a year, Lucy's life was completely different. Her therapist taught her how important it was to love herself— after teaching her what love was in the first place. Lucy had a new foster family that treated her kindly, respectfully, and showered her with genuine affection and love. It took a long time, but Lucy finally did learn to love herself. It was her first step to taking back her power from the negativity she grew up in.

Loving yourself isn't selfish; in fact, it is one of the most selfless acts you can perform. A human being cannot survive without love, especially the love given to oneself. And you know what can't survive in the presence of love? Negative self-talk. Start tearing through the negative self-talk as it comes to mind. Identify it, figure out what it is trying to accomplish, then put it on the ground and say, "You aren't welcome here. You can't survive when I love myself!"

As you start actively loving yourself, you will discover amazing things! You'll start to recognize when you achieve something you've worked hard for. You'll start to appreciate the people around you who love you unconditionally. You'll notice that when you look in the mirror, your first thoughts aren't negative self-talk.

Loving yourself is also more than a state of mind. Love is an action. Ask yourself, "What can I do to show myself love that I might not have considered before?" This can be any number of things:

- Take that vacation you always wanted to the beach.
- Go to the spa for a massage.
- Get tickets for that show you've missed three times.
- Go see a movie with your partner.
- Try a new sport.

- Learn a new musical instrument.
- Invite friends over for a cookout.
- Go to the annual office holiday party.
- Apply for that promotion.

What those things have in common is that you haven't done them because negative self-talk has beaten you down and made you believe you don't deserve to do any of those things, or that if you do those things, you will be judged and laughed at. Take back your power by taking action! Show yourself acts of love!

Believe it or not, the study from 2016 mentioned earlier also suggested that "love is one of the most valuable intentional emotional experiences humans can produce to drive brain plasticity in a positive direction" (Shaffer, 2016). How about that? Science is telling us that loving yourself is essential for engaging neuroplasticity! Self-love is the ultimate tool for starting this amazing process, and rewiring your brain through neuroplasticity is not only possible—it's achievable!

Another way to take back your power is to fight this common thread of negative self-talk: "You are so worthless." "You don't have anything to offer anyone." "You're spineless and brainless and could never help anyone with anything." Our worth is found not only within but also by sharing our love and positive energy with others. The dictionary definition of being worthy is "having or showing the qualities or abilities that merit recognition." It is quite easy for negative self-talk to beat that back. How? It keeps you from getting out in your community and doing things with and for others.

Think about a time you wanted to help with a community project or volunteer at a charitable event. Maybe you've always wanted to go on a mission trip with your church or donate an hour of your time at the local food bank. What's been stopping you?

"Don't bother," says negative self-talk, "because no one wants you there anyway. How could you possibly be a help? You'll just get in the way because you don't know what you're doing."

I've got news for you. NST is wrong. Do yourself a favor. Right now, put this book down and write out three things you've always wanted to help out with in your community. Don't let NST stop you! Write them down.

Did you write down more than three? I sure hope so! Okay, the next step is to get online and find out when and where those opportunities exist. Don't the people you want to help deserve your time and effort? Of course they do! They are human beings just like you who have had a run of bad luck, or maybe they are trying to get out of a bad situation. Don't you deserve to help them? Absolutely! Go find those opportunities and write down the information next to each one. I'll wait.

Great job! Let's move to the next step: What skills or special meaning can you bring to each opportunity? Shut down your NST and think about it. What unique thing do you bring to each opportunity? Even if you have no experience, but passion, that's a plus. Take back your power and stand up for yourself! Write down what you can bring in the commission of each opportunity.

Awesome! Now it's time to take back your power in the most effective way of all: sign up to work those opportunities! Contact whom you need to, or sign up online— either way, don't let NST talk you out of it. Every time your NST starts in, stop it in its tracks and simply say, "No, you're wrong. I can do this. I *will* do this."

When you work to love yourself and find value and worth in what you bring to the community, you are taking effective steps to quiet the negative voice.

Chapter 11: Quiet the Negative Voice

When you have struggled with negative self-talk for years, it becomes difficult to accept the silence that remains once you have control over NST. Any kind of major change in your thinking will provoke a mental and physical response. When you make a change, you are upsetting the homeostasis—the status quo—and NST *does not* like that. It knows that when you start moving away from it, its power is being taken away too.

The human body will always instinctively react against something that changes the status quo—it wants to keep the current balance, even if that state is heavy with negativity. I won't lie to you: getting rid of your negative self-talk and rewiring your brain will create a sense of upheaval. But you know what? That's okay. Things in our lives, and in this world, never stay exactly the same. Every day is new. Every minute is different. Every step we take toward a better life and better state of mind is a step we've never taken. Is it a little scary? Yes. Is it worth it? *One hundred percent yes!*

Once you get the upper hand over negative self-talk, your mind might be a little quieter than you're used to. There will be a void that begs to be filled. Aristotle said, "Nature abhors a vacuum," meaning that empty or unfilled places are not natural. We can feel that when someone we love has passed away. The empty space they leave behind is painful, and we seek to fill it. So what steps can you take to satisfy the needs of nature?

One way to fill that void is with positive self-talk. "Researchers continue to explore the effects of positive thinking and optimism on health. Health benefits that positive thinking may provide include:

- Increased life span
- Lower rates of depression
- Lower levels of distress
- Greater resistance to the common cold
- Better psychological and physical well-being
- Better cardiovascular health and reduced risk of death from cardiovascular disease
- Better coping skills during hardships and times of stress

It's unclear why people who engage in positive thinking experience these health benefits. One theory is that having a positive outlook enables you to cope better with stressful situations" (Sparks, 2019).

Being better able to cope with stress is one way we beat back negative self-talk. Coping skills are essential in making any significant transformation of the mind. There are different categories of coping skills, but since we are talking about rewiring the brain, let's look at a list of cognitive coping skills (skills of the mind):

- Make a gratitude list
- Brainstorm solutions
- Lower your expectations of the situation
- Keep an inspirational quote with you
- Be flexible
- Write a list of goals
- Take a class

- Act opposite of negative feelings
- Write a list of pros and cons for decisions
- Reward or pamper yourself when successful
- Write a list of strengths
- Accept a challenge with a positive attitude (Flannery, 2021)

Each one of these skills is a fantastic way to overcome negative self-talk. When you busy yourself with positive activities that allow you to explore your talents and express yourself without reservation, you are quieting the negative voice. It doesn't have any room in your brain anymore; you've taken its power.

Now, someone who has lived with NST for a lifetime might have feelings of guilt or self-indulgence when looking at this list. You are not being selfish in trying to improve the environment of your mind! You are taking the necessary steps to be healthy, find your power, and take back your life from negative self-talk!

You've taken back your power. You've quieted the negative voice. Are you ready for the challenge? It's time to rewire your brain.

Chapter 12: Consciously Rewire Your Brain

Remember, the concept of neuroplasticity is "the ability of the nervous system to respond to intrinsic or extrinsic stimuli by reorganizing its structure, function, and connections" (Cramer et al., 2011). Basically, it is the ability to consciously rewire your brain. Scientists have been studying this phenomenon for decades, trying to find ways to use neuroplasticity to help patients with mental health issues, degenerative brain diseases, or even brain cancer. If a human being were able to consciously control how the structure of the brain is maintained and changed, he or she would be able to rewire their brain to stop negative self-talk altogether!

The National Institutes of Health Blueprint for Neuroscience Research sponsored a workshop in 2009. Basic and clinical researchers in disciplines from central nervous system injury/stroke, mental/addictive disorders, pediatric/developmental disorders, and neurodegeneration/ageing identified cardinal examples of neuroplasticity, underlying mechanisms, therapeutic implications, and common denominators. Promising therapies that may enhance training-induced cognitive and motor learning, such as brain stimulation and neuropharmacological interventions, were identified, along with questions of how best to use this body of information to reduce human disability. Improved understanding of adaptive mechanisms at every level, from molecules to synapses, to networks, to behaviour, can be gained from iterative collaborations between basic and clinical researchers. (Cramer et al., 2011).

What does all that scientific babble mean? Scientists are looking for ways to "train" the brain. They are currently exploring "brain stimulation," which would require a laboratory with special equipment to monitor brain activity (electroencephalogram, MRI, fMRI, etc.) while the training was taking place. "Neuropharmacological interventions" would indicate the use of chemicals—medications or experimental drugs—that would require scientific observation to determine their success.

In the diagram below, neurology researchers based at UC Irvine in California attempt to present a visual framework for the use of neuroplasticity in behavioral modification within the brain. The cycle begins with identifying which types of brain behaviors can be part of neurofeedback training while utilizing neuroplasticity. The researchers then present the three primary levels of neuroplasticity, which in turn lead to the possible interventions for various clinical conditions. Finally, the researchers present the two mechanisms of assessment after treatment.

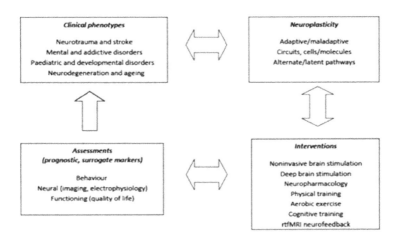

Conceptual overview of the relationship between clinical phenotypes, neuroplasticity, therapeutic interventions, and assessment of function. (Cramer et al., 2011)

Although we have to admit, as the researchers do, that some of this material is based on hypothesis, these discoveries and assumptions are being considered the basis for cognitive training of the brain. The researchers state that cognitive training is "a direct extension of physical therapy to the non-motor aspects of the human brain and so has been examined across a number of disease conditions. However, the complexities of the distributed neural systems that underlie human behavioral syndromes introduce unique challenges for the design (creation) of effective interventions . . . Evidence suggests that, as individuals learn to modify their cognitive representations and behavioral responses to distressing stimuli, widespread changes occur in frontal cognitive control systems and in limbic system activation" (Goldapple et al., 2004; Kennedy et al., 2007; and Farb et al., 2010, qtd. in Cramer et al., 2011).

These findings are exciting! Researchers are telling us that neurofeedback, when combined with harnessing neuroplasticity, will allow humans to retrain their brains. Rewiring your brain is no longer science fiction—it is possible! Science is telling us that there are specific steps we need to take to be successful at rewiring our brains. The next section is a step-by-step process that combines all that we have learned here to create a process for rewiring our brains to stop negative self-talk.

Chapter 13: The Process

Step 1: Recognize Negative Self-Talk

In part I, we talked about recognizing the negative voice, identifying it, and acknowledging the problem.

Journaling

For approximately seven days, make your best effort at writing down any negative self-talk that comes to mind. You need to write it *all* down. It is also helpful to write the day, date, time, and location when the NST occurred. All of those things are relevant if we are going to stop NST and rewire our brains for life without it. But once you have written down an NST thought, *do not go back to it* for at least seven days. When you write it down, you are tossing it in the garbage for disposal. You don't need to review it until you are ready for the next step.

Here is a brief example of one day's journal:

Monday – April 5, 2021
0730 – got out of bed, walked to the bathroom, looked in the mirror and thought, "Jeez, you need to lose some weight, fatty!" I grabbed my belly and agreed.
0815 – was walking to my car when I realized I forgot my lunch bag. "Stupid! Why are you such a forgetful idiot?" I shook my head and thought about it while I walked back to my apartment to grab my lunch.
1004 – my boss stopped by my desk and praised me for my latest presentation. He told me that I made him, and the rest

of the department, look so good that he was going to put through the raise I was to get next month right away. "It's just a pity raise. Anyone in the department could've done what you did."

1211 – I opened my lunch bag in the employee cafeteria and pulled out my sandwich, chips, and apple. I grabbed a soda from the nearby vending machine. As I popped the top, I heard, "Chips and a soda? What did we talk about this morning, fatty?"

1456 – I am so sleepy; I am about to drop my head to my desk. Why does this always happen around 3 in the afternoon? "Because you had too many carbs for lunch, you moron! If you ate better, this would stop!"

1730 – I ran into the restaurant to meet my boyfriend for dinner. I apologized for being late. I had a late conference call. He replied with a smile, "That's okay. I understand, and you texted me, so no big deal." I put down my bag, lifted the menu to cover my face, and heard, "Sure, sure, it's okay! He's not really into you. He's just stringing you along because he feels sorry for you."

2140 – I am brushing my teeth before going to bed and glance up to see my reflection in the mirror. All I hear is, "Fatty, fatty, fatty! You can brush and groom all you want, but it won't hide all that blubber!"

2200 – As I pull up the covers and switch off the lights, I sigh. It's dark, I'm tired. "How can you be tired? You sat on your fat ass all day!"

These are eight instances of negative self-talk in a roughly 18-hour period. Do you think there were probably more? There is no question there were. Journaling doesn't just require the discipline to stop and write things down—it takes courage to write them *all* down. Be honest with yourself: How many instances of NST do you think you will leave out when you start journaling? You get tired of it because every time you write one of these down, you will experience pain.

Who wants to be in pain all day? No one does. But the only way to get past it is through openly accepting your memories, acknowledging your past, and knowing that it's a process that does have an end—you can't get past your negative self-talk until you walk through the pain. It may not feel like it right now, but negative self-talk can be beaten if you have the bravery and brawn to walk through its fire.

Therapists, psychiatrists, and counselors of every stripe have been recommending journaling as a therapeutic tool for decades. Why? Because it works. "Keeping a journal helps you create order when your world feels like it's in chaos. You get to know yourself by revealing your most private fears, thoughts, and feelings. Look at your writing time as personal relaxation time. It's a time when you can de-stress and wind down. Write in a place that's relaxing and soothing, maybe with a cup of tea. Look forward to your journaling time. And know that you're doing something good for your mind and body" (Health, 2021).

Once you have journaled for seven days, it's time to go back and read through your negative self-talk. It is not unusual to feel pain during this review—if you take the attitude that you are reading about your failures as a human being.

If you want it to instead be a learning experience, remember what we said at the beginning: treat each entry like trash that needs to be tossed out. But before you take out the trash, search for repetition of certain phrases or voices, certain times of day that NST seems to dominate, or specific activities that trigger your NST.

Write a paragraph analyzing what you learned from your journaling. Consider the following questions:

- What time of day am I most likely to experience negative self-talk?
- Is there a particular day of the week that was worse than others? Why?
- Is there a dominant voice among all the NST? Who is it?
- What phrases do I hear repeatedly?
- Which phrases cause the most pain?
- What memories are attached to those phrases specifically?
- What are my triggers? Do they involve people, places, things, times, events?
- Are the NST thoughts invading every hour of my day, or just when I'm communicating with others?
- Do I talk back to them? (Believe it or not, most people do.)
- Did I try to fight back, or did I just accept the NST as truth?
- How did each instance affect my mood?

It's amazing what we can learn when we go back and walk through all the negative self-talk we hear in a week. "Keeping a journal allows you to track patterns, trends and improvements over time. When current circumstances appear insurmountable, you can look back on previous dilemmas that you have since resolved and learn from them. You might also encounter moments where you feel confused and uncertain about your feelings. By writing them down, you're able to tap into your internal world and better make sense of things" (Sehgal and Chopra, 2019).

Doing an analysis of your NST journal is exactly what we are talking about here: finding the patterns in the chaos, learning from past mistakes, or making sense of things that never made sense before. "When you encounter a difficult problem, removing the situation from your mind and putting it down on paper encourages you to look at things from different angles and brainstorm several solutions in a more organized manner. Writing in your journal as a way to release and express your thoughts, feelings, and emotions can be a life-changing habit" (Sehgal & Chopra, 2019).

When you are analyzing your journal, you can take one of two approaches: narrative or investigative.

Narrative

By definition, a narrative is the telling of a story. Who are the main characters? Where does the plot take place? Are there multiple settings and events? When does the plot begin? What are the rising and falling actions of the story? What are the pivotal moments? What is the ultimate resolution?

If you have a more creative mind, writing out your NST week as a narrative could be a very healthy way to analyze what's been going on in your head. Create a list of characters— yourself, the voices, and anyone you interacted with during NST. Define the settings of the story and include visual descriptions using colors, textures, and objects (for example, a sterile office building or a breezy park with lots of prickly pine trees). What should your plot be? What events do you need to include (hint: all of them)? When did you have your pivotal moment, and what was it? Was there an ultimate resolution?

The next section is the previous one-day journal example, now explored in a narrative format.

Jenny's Day

The alarm went off at 7:30 am, as usual, and I got out of bed. I plodded across the carpet to the bathroom, glanced in the mirror, and a lady said, "Jeez, you need to lose some weight, fatty!" I grabbed my belly and agreed with her. I searched the closet for my fat clothes, decided I could afford to skip breakfast, and grabbed my keys and purse. I was walking to my car when I realized I forgot my lunch bag.

"Stupid! Why are you such a forgetful idiot?" he said. I shook my head and thought about it while I walked back to my apartment to grab my lunch.

Despite a fairly boring morning, my boss stopped by my desk around 10:00 am and praised me for my latest presentation. He told me that I made him, and the rest of the department, look so good that he was going to put through the raise I was to get next month right away. I grinned from ear to ear—I really needed the money! Then the voice whispered, "It's just a pity raise. Anyone in the department could've done what you did." I thought about that as I finished my morning work. I couldn't wait for the distraction of lunchtime.

Around noon, I opened my lunch bag in the employee cafeteria and pulled out my sandwich, chips, and apple. I grabbed a soda from the nearby vending machine. As I popped the top, I heard her say, "Chips and a soda? What did we talk about this morning, fatty?" Now, I was angry. I took a huge swig and thought to her, "Shut up! Screw you! I can do what I want!" I finished my lunch in relative peace and quiet, sighing with a hint of relief. Too soon, it was time to go back to my desk and start the afternoon stretch.

Just before 3:00 pm, I crashed—hard. I was so sleepy; I was about to drop my head to my desk. Why does this always happen around three in the afternoon? I wondered. "Because you had too many carbs for lunch, you moron! If you ate better, this would stop!" That drill sergeant needed to get off my back about my food, but he was right. I was ready to head home and clean up for a dinner date with my boyfriend when my boss pulled me into a conference call—a call that went on and on. I couldn't stop looking at the time, and eventually I had to text my boyfriend that I was running late.

At 5:30 pm, I ran into the restaurant to meet my boyfriend for dinner. I apologized for being late. He replied with a smile as he pulled my chair out for me, "That's okay. I understand, and you texted me, so no big deal." As I put down my bag, he planted a sweet kiss on my forehead. I lifted the menu to cover my face and heard, "Sure, sure, it's okay! He's not really into you. He's just stringing you along because he feels sorry for you." I pushed the thought back and tried to focus on having a good time with my man.

After a lovely date, he dropped me off at my door and kissed me good night. I waved as he drove away and then let myself into the apartment. I dropped my stuff on the floor, exhausted from a very long day. I was brushing my teeth before going to bed and glanced up to see my reflection in the mirror. All I heard was, "Fatty, fatty, fatty! You can brush and groom all you want, but it won't hide all that blubber!" I took a pointed look at my belly and thighs and butt. *How much of that was true?* I sighed and crawled into my bed—alone. As I pulled up the covers and switched off the light, I sighed. It's dark, I'm tired, and I really don't need her to tell me, "How can you be tired? You sat on your fat ass all day!"

Though this seems like an almost verbatim recitation of the journal, there are some key points that need to be made.

1. Jenny assigned a gender to each voice, meaning she has an idea of who is talking negatively at that point.
2. When told about her raise, Jenny was quite happy until the NST voice dragged her down, and then she allowed it to dominate the rest of her morning.
3. During lunch, Jenny yelled back at the voice. She took back her power for that moment, and for the rest of her lunchtime, she was able to relax and feel a bit relieved.
4. During the sleepy time NST attack, Jenny tacitly referred to the voice as the drill sergeant and made the mental statement that he needed to back off—a step in the right direction.
5. During dinner, Jenny didn't allow herself to appreciate and enjoy the affections of her boyfriend because of the NST, even though she tried hard to push it back.
6. At bedtime, Jenny again faced the voice that repeated *fatty, fatty*, and she started asking herself how much of it was true?

Within Jenny's story are victories and slipups. By reviewing her day, she can see when she was strong enough to fight back and when she allowed negative self-talk to interrupt and control her life.

Is that a common thing with you? Do you allow NST to interrupt and control your life in any way? Are there times when it is easier to fight back? These are all a part of the method to identify and process every instance of negative self-talk you have in a given day. If you are more of a logical thinker, the investigative analysis would probably be more useful.

Investigative

An investigative analysis will have you pulling out the instances of negative self-talk, one by one, and categorizing them. This is most easily done with a table or chart.

<u>Who is Talking to You?</u>

Your analysis of a week's worth of negative self-talk leaves you with little doubt about who is speaking to you and what memories are fueling that negative self-talk. "Many different views exist about the origins of the nature of our internal dialogue . . . and many experts claim our self-talk mirrors the way we were spoken to and dealt with as children . . . As children, we learned to internalize the messages our parents sent us, for better or for worse, as a survival strategy. For example, as children, it's best that we internalize messages such as 'Don't run out into the street.' However, those messages that sound more like 'You're worthy of love and acceptance only when you accomplish something' don't do us any favors, either as children or later as adults" (Norris, 2018).

This research suggests that our parents are probably the primary voices we hear in negative self-talk. As children we crave their love and acceptance, and we want them to be proud of us. But parents, just like anyone else, can say things in the heat of the moment that they don't mean. That can set us up for some negative self-talk because children don't have the capacity to differentiate between words spoken in anger and words spoken in love. Their brains simply record the information and store the memories.

As we grow and begin to interact with others, those voices can also feed our memory banks. Remember when we talked about the brain and how the prefrontal cortex doesn't fully evolve until adulthood? Even though children continue to mature and grow throughout their childhood and adolescence, their ability to separate words continues to be a simple recording process. As such, anyone who bullies us will have a voice in our negative self-talk arena. Our brains simply store the data. Those incidents also have long-term effects when it comes to how we see ourselves, and thus how we form our negative self-talk.

The experience of being bullied can end up causing lasting damage to victims. This is both self-evident, and also supported by an increasing body of research. It is not necessary to be physically harmed in order to suffer lasting harm. Words and gestures are quite enough. What is far more difficult to mend is the primary wound that bullying victims suffer which is damage to their self-concepts, to their identities. Being the repetitive target of bullying damages your ability to view yourself as a desirable, capable, and effective individual. There are two ugly outcomes that stem from learning to view yourself as a less than desirable, incapable individual. The first ugly outcome is that it becomes more likely that you will become increasingly susceptible to becoming depressed and/or angry and/or bitter. Being bullied teaches you that you are undesirable, that you are not safe in the world, and (when it is dished out by forces that are physically superior to yourself) that you are relatively powerless to defend yourself. The second outcome unfolds more slowly over time. Having a wounded self-concept makes it harder for you to believe in yourself, and when you have difficulty believing in yourself, you will tend to have a harder time persevering through difficult situations and challenging circumstances. (American, 2020)

Go back to your seven-day journal. Review your narrative or investigative analysis. Write a list here of whom you have identified in your NST, what they said, and what part of you that hurts (physical appearance, intelligence, self-worth, etc.). There are 10 entries available, but you may have more or less than that:

Voice 1 belongs to _____.
_____ said _____
_____
_____
_____
_____. What _____ said hurt me
_____. It made me feel like _____
_____
_____

_____

_____

_____.

Voice 2 belongs to _____.

_____ said _____

_____

_____

_____. What _____ said hurt me

_____. It made me feel like _____

_____

_____

_____

_____

_____.

Voice 3 belongs to _____.

_____ said _____

_____

_____

_____. What _____ said hurt me

_____. It made me feel like _____

_____

_____

_____

_____

_____.

Voice 4 belongs to _____.

_____ said _____

_____

_____

_____

_____. What _____ said hurt me

_____. It made me feel like _____

_____

_____

_____

_____

_____.

Voice 5 belongs to _____.

_____ said _____

_____

_____

_____

_____. What _____ said hurt me

_____. It made me feel like _____

_____

_____

_____

_____

_____.

Voice 6 belongs to _____.

_____ said _____

_____

_____

_____

_____. What _____ said hurt me

_____. It made me feel like _____

_____

_____

_____

_____

_____.

Voice 7 belongs to _____.

_____ said _____

_____

_____

_____. What _____ said hurt me

_____. It made me feel like _____

_____

_____

_____

_____

_____.

Voice 8 belongs to _____.

_____ said _____

_____

_____

_____. What _____ said hurt me

_____. It made me feel like _____

_____

_____

_____

_____.

Voice 9 belongs to _____.

_____ said _____

_____

_____

_____

_____. What _____ said hurt me

_____. It made me feel like _____

_____

_____

_____

_____

_____.

Voice 10 belongs to _____.

_____ said _____

_____

_____

_____

_____. What _____ said hurt me

_____. It made me feel like _____

_____

_____

_____

_____

_____.

After reviewing each of these different voices, do you think you can forgive the person who hurt you? Think about a few things: When did it happen? Why did it happen? Where did it happen? If you have an NST voice of your mom telling you that you need to lose weight, think about why she may have said that. Was she worried about your health, or was she commenting about your looks? If you were 10 years old and had recently gained a significant amount of weight for no apparent reason, she was probably worried about your health.

If you were 15 and your mom wanted you to start dating and have more friends—like she did at your age—it could have been about your looks. Parents want us to have the same fun experiences they had as teens, and if we aren't, they may look for any reason why it isn't happening and then focus on that. In this case, the comment was about *her* more than it was about you. It was about the life she wanted for you and how she believed that should look.

It's not unusual for offhand comments or direct digs at you to be about insecurities the person has regarding him or herself. There are different reasons why people bully, including the following:

- wanting to dominate others and improve their social status
- having low self-esteem
- having a lack of remorse or failing to recognize their behavior as a problem
- feeling angry or frustrated
- struggling socially
- being the victim of bullying themselves

Some children who bully may enjoy getting their own way. Others may like conflict and aggression. Some may be thoughtless, rather than deliberately hurtful. Some may have difficulties with health, schoolwork, and self-esteem. And some may be emotionally neglected, bullied, abused, or be experiencing violence themselves. (Health Direct, n.d.)

When you think about how the minds of bullies work, you can almost feel sorry for them. In a sense, they are in pain and don't know how to handle it, so they lash out at others they determine would be just as vulnerable as they feel. It is a way for them to feel stronger, more powerful, and less helpless.

Go back to your list of voices. One by one, think about each voice, the situation when the negative self-talk occurred, and how old you were. Do you honestly believe they intended to harm you? Is it possible they were simply saying something they thought was helpful but that your brain stored as a negative event? Was this person bullying you to lash out from a personal hurt they couldn't handle anymore? Don't just give it a quick review. *Think* about it. Process it. Consider all the angles. Think about them, not you. After you have considered each one, complete the following exercise in forgiveness:

Forgiveness Exercise: If we hope to grow and change and rewire our brains, we have to employ the act of forgiveness. "Forgiveness means different things to different people. Generally, however, it involves a decision to let go of resentment and thoughts of revenge. The act that hurt or offended you might always be with you, but forgiveness can lessen its grip on you and help free you from the control of the person who harmed you. Forgiveness can even lead to feelings of understanding, empathy, and compassion for the one who hurt you. Forgiveness doesn't mean forgetting or excusing the harm done to you or making up with the person who caused the harm. Forgiveness brings a kind of peace that helps you go on with life" (Adult, 2021).

Voice 1 belongs to _____._____ said

_____

_____

_____

_____

_____

_____. _____ said this because

_____

_____

_____

_____

_____

_____

_____.

I can forgive _____ because he/she

_____

_____

_____

_____

_____ and forgiving him/her is my first step in rewiring my brain to stop negative self-talk.

Voice 2 belongs to _____._____ said

_____

_____

_____

_____

_____

_____. _____ said this because

_____

_____

_____

_____

_____

_____

_____

_____.

I can forgive _____ because he/she

_____

_____

_____

_____

_____

_____ and forgiving him/her is my first step in rewiring my brain to stop negative self-talk.

Voice 3 belongs to _____._____ said

_____

_____

_____

_____

_____. _____ said this because

_____

_____

_____

_____

_____

_____

_____

_____.

I can forgive _____ because he/she

_____

_____

_____

_____

_____ and forgiving him/her is my first step in
rewiring my brain to stop negative self-talk.

Voice 4 belongs to _____._____ said

_____

_____

_____

_____. _____ said this because

_____

_____

_____

_____

_____

_____

_____.

I can forgive _____ because he/she

_____

_____

_____

_____

_____ and forgiving him/her is my first step in rewiring my brain to stop negative self-talk.

Voice 5 belongs to _____._____ said

_____

_____

_____

_____

_____

_____. _____ said this because

_____

_____

_____

_____

_____

_____

_____.

I can forgive _____ because he/she

_____

_____

_____

_____

_____

_____ and forgiving him/her is my first step in rewiring my brain to stop negative self-talk.

Voice 6 belongs to _____._____ said

_____

_____

_____

_____

_____

_____. _____ said this because

_____

_____

_____

_____

_____

_____

_____

_____.

I can forgive _____ because he/she

_____

_____

_____

_____

_____ and forgiving him/her is my first step in rewiring my brain to stop negative self-talk.

Voice 7 belongs to _____. _____ said

_____

_____

_____

_____

_____. _____ said this because

_____

_____

_____

_____

_____

_____

_____.

I can forgive _____ because he/she

_____

_____

_____

_____

_____ and forgiving him/her is my first step in rewiring my brain to stop negative self-talk.

Voice 8 belongs to _____._____ said

_____

_____

_____

_____

_____. _____ said this because

_____

_____

_____

_____

_____

_____

_____.

I can forgive _____ because he/she

_____

_____

_____

_____

_____ and forgiving him/her is my first step in rewiring my brain to stop negative self-talk.

Voice 9 belongs to _____. _____ said

_____

_____

_____

_____

_____

_____. _____ said this because

_____

_____

_____

_____

_____

_____

_____.

I can forgive _____ because he/she

_____

_____

_____

_____

_____ and forgiving him/her is my first step in rewiring my brain to stop negative self-talk.

Voice 10 belongs to _____. _____ said

_____

_____

_____

_____

_____

_____. _____ said this because

_____

_____

_____

_____

_____

_____

_____.

I can forgive _____ because he/she

_____

_____

_____

_____

_____ and forgiving him/her is my first step in rewiring my brain to stop negative self-talk.

This part of the process is the most difficult emotionally. Letting go of our burdens makes us realize that we have spent years allowing the words of others to control our emotions, our reactions to situations, and our views of ourselves. It's okay to get angry. It's okay to be upset about the lost time. But don't dwell on it. The last step in the forgiveness exercise is the most important:

I forgive myself. I am starting fresh. I have a new life. I am worthy. I am beautiful. I have a positive and glorious future ahead. I will no longer allow the past to determine my present.

All of the work you have done here can be exhausting. Don't move forward without taking at least a day to process, meditate or pray, and emotionally recover. Only when you are in a good place mentally is it time to move on to the next step of rewiring your brain.

Mute NST

You have done some great work so far! If you have made it to this point in the process, you are doing awesome! Because negative self-talk is such an emotion-based event, getting through the emotional healing will take time. You may think, "Wait a minute; I thought we were done?" No, not yet. The emotional portion is the most difficult because you have to revisit so much pain and deal with people you love deeply, know well, may dislike, or even have deep hatred for. Now it is time for the next step—the analytical.

We know that our thoughts come from a combination of stimulus and memory. As we learn every day, we are adding new memories. Have you ever considered that the learning process is about memory? As we learn to read, write, do math, practice art, participate in sports, do a job, and function in a relationship, it is *all* about memory.

"Learning and memory are cognitive functions that encompass a variety of parts. These parts can be structured in different ways. For example, we can focus on time, or differentiate memory by content or how the information was acquired (see a flowchart of the various processes in the figure below). It seems clear that the cognitive structure of learning and memory is complex. It is also clear that memory is tightly connected to time perception, attention, and emotional value of memory contents" (Brem et al., 2014).

138

So our ability to learn is directly related to the same brain processes that store memories. While the figure below is a good indicator of how complicated the process actually is (the various types of memory and different ways to learn), it's enough to have the knowledge so we can use the tools to help us separate our daily learned thoughts necessary for function from the event-driven thoughts of negative self-talk.

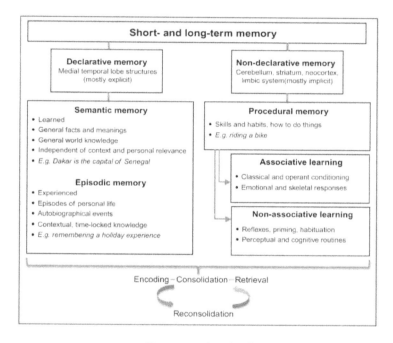

(Brem et al., 2014)

From this chart, we know that episodic memory is where we find the bases for negative self-talk. It is centered around events - episodes in our personal lives - and time-based events. Our daily thoughts directly related to function and process are located in the non-declarative, procedural memory.

Clearly, we cannot simply push an area on our head to "activate" these centers. They are always working, 24/7, and it will take practice to isolate only those memories and skills we need to perform our daily activities. But how do we practice that? How do we practice accessing only a portion of our memories purposefully?

Over years of research, empirical tests have shown the cognitive and social psychological evidence does support the existence of unconscious mental activity and its potential to impact judgments and behavior. "Unconscious conflict resolution processes thus furnish valuable information to conscious processes of planning for the future. Given sufficiently strong motivations and commitment to the planned course of action, specific plans such as 'when X happens, I will do Y' themselves operate automatically when the future opportunity arises" (Bargh and Morsella, 2008).

When our unconscious mind feeds us negative self-talk, our brains will eventually re-route or even destroy negative self-talk *before it even enters our consciousness*, if we have the motivation and commitment to change the course. Again, it will take lots of practice and mindfulness to achieve this, but isn't having a happy life, with no NST, worth the effort?

Step 2: Conventional Methods

Standing Up for Yourself

When we talked about bullies, we mentioned that most of them bully because they themselves are hurting in some way. We learn very young that the quickest way to stop a bully is to stand up to him or her. Bullies are already feeling vulnerable when they are bullying you, so if you stand up to them, they will have a flight response and likely back down. If they experience a fight response, I hope you have your fists ready.

Let's begin by creating what we will call your Positive Response. Our goal here is to create a brief phrase or sentence that helps remind you of your inner strength and helps you take the extra step of standing up to your negative self-talk. Start by making a list of your attributes. What are you good at? What do you excel at? What do people tell you is a positive character trait?

All About Me

Things I Am Good At
Things People Like About Me
Areas I Excel In

_____

_____

_____

_____

_____

_____

_____

_____

_____

_____

_____

_____

_____

_____

_____

_____

_____

Now that your list is done, pick two or three things that make you smile. What on your list is the most appealing to you? What gives you the biggest confidence boost? Let's look at a couple of examples that might be helpful to you:

- *I am a wonderful mother, wife, and teacher that you cannot touch with your negativity.*
- *My intelligence and wit cannot be bothered by your petty insignificance.*
- *You can't win a battle against my skills and experience in war.*
- *Your small and trivial words are no match for my education and joy of life.*
- *My powerful singing voice will always drown out your tiny words.*

From here, you need to create your own Positive Response. Don't just jump at the first thing that comes to mind. Really think about what it will take for you to stand up to your negative self-talk and beat it into submission.

My Positive Response:

_____
_____
_____
_____
_____
_____
_____.

Congratulations! You have created the first tool you need to start rewiring your brain! You've found your powerful, unbeatable voice, and negative self-talk can take a hike! Now don't make the mistake of being afraid to say your words out loud—even in public. Maybe you shouldn't shout it from the rooftops, as that could confuse and scare people, but there is nothing wrong with stopping for a moment and repeating your Positive Response until NST goes back into its hiding place.

Practice this response until you have it memorized. In fact, while you are memorizing it, imagine it taking the place of some piece of negative self-talk that lingers in your mind. Picture your words kicking NST to the curb with as much force as you can. Your mind is very powerful—turn that power against NST and make it work for your good health and well-being!

Finding Support

It's not unusual for people who experience a lot of negative self-talk to need just a bit more help in finding their voice and gaining the strength to stand up. This is where therapy or a recovery group makes the most sense.

Therapy is not for everyone—we can't stress that enough—but that doesn't mean you should automatically write it off. Many organizations offer one free session or a free consultation to help you determine if individual therapy is right for you. For some people, the idea of sitting in a room sharing hurts and painful memories with a virtual stranger is frightening or unsettling. That is a normal human reaction. We don't want to appear weak or helpless in front of others.

However, therapists, psychiatrists, psychologists, and counselors have all been trained to help you work through that initial discomfort and find the value in talking out the things that bother you the most. When you attend your first session, the therapist will ask questions about you and your life. This helps them make an initial assessment of your situation. Questions could be about why you sought therapy, your personal history and current situation, your life, your family history, physical or mental symptoms you may be experiencing, and your current home situation. The therapist uses this information to better understand your problem (Bressert, 2016).

Be prepared—disclosing some of this information could be painful. Don't worry if you feel like crying. That's okay. Therapy is a safe space where no one else can see you break down and go through hurts and pains that you have allowed to take up valuable space in your heart and mind. This is your chance to throw negative self-talk under the bus and start getting it under better control.

And remember that therapy is a team effort. Be an active participant. Don't sit by while your therapist talks— remain open and answer the therapist's questions with total honesty. Don't be afraid to ask questions either. Therapists are some of the greatest people on the planet to ask questions of. They have no agenda. They aren't part of your family. They are completely objective and can see things for what they truly are (Bressert, 2016).

If therapy doesn't sound like something that you are comfortable with, the next option is to try a recovery group. There were several that we mentioned in Part III, but most of them have similar formats and the same mission: they are there to help people find relief from pain and to create a new path to follow for a healthier life—mentally, emotionally, physically, and spiritually. There are many benefits to participating in a support group, including the following:

- Feeling less lonely, isolated, or judged
- Reducing distress, depression, anxiety, or fatigue
- Talking openly and honestly about your feelings
- Improving skills to cope with challenges
- Staying motivated to manage chronic health conditions
- Gaining a sense of empowerment, control, or hope
- Learning about health, economic, or social resources (Mayo, 2021)

When you consider all the potential benefits of these groups, can you really afford *not* to try it out? Recovery groups come in all shapes and sizes, and there is a fit for everyone.

Recovery groups can be small (20–30 people) or very large (150–200 people). If you have trouble being around strangers, find a local group with a smaller attendance level. Then you won't be as intimidated by the size of the program or the number of strangers you will have to have contact with.

But if you are all about people, a larger group would be a great choice. The larger programs also tend to have more options for group meetings and special studies outside the program, and they provide the opportunity to create lasting bonds with people who can help guide you on your journey.

To get the most out of a recovery group, it is best to begin by embracing the mission and principles it is founded on. If at your first meeting, it doesn't seem like a good fit, don't get discouraged. There are other groups and other meetings out there. Groups like SMART and Celebrate Recovery have multiple meetings of differing sizes in most medium- to large-sized cities.

Once you've selected a recovery program, the people there are your greatest support system. They can become like your second family. If your negative self-talk is very much driven by family or family events, this is your chance to get support from others who will take great care with you and be there for you when you need them the most. And you might be surprised to find out how many of them face negative self-talk just like you do!

"Support groups bring together people who are going through or have gone through similar experiences. For example, this common ground might be addiction, chronic medical conditions, mental health issues, bereavement, or caregiving. The common experience among members of a support group often means they have similar feelings, worries, everyday problems, treatment decisions or treatment side effects. Participating in a group provides you with an opportunity to be with people who are likely to have a common purpose and likely to understand one another. A support group provides an opportunity for people to share personal experiences and feelings, coping strategies, or firsthand stories about their own experiences" (Mayo, 2021).

Whether you choose individual therapy or a recovery group, you need support. The process of rewiring your brain is not going to be easy, and you will need people to lean on. They can be there to offer you advice, to listen, to walk through tough times together, or to help you get mental health treatment if need be.

When you start focusing on rewiring your brain, you will be spending a lot of time alone in quiet spaces. That can lead to a feeling of isolation, and that could potentially trigger more negative self-talk. Let a friend or your therapist know what it is you are trying to achieve. Explain how NST has affected your life and how you are trying to use mindfulness, science, and anything else that might help to alter your thought processes. Share this book with them if they have questions about the process or techniques offered.

Step 3: Nonconventional Methods

Retrain Your Brain

We've gone through a lot of scientific material about how the brain functions. We learned that our prefrontal cortex (a portion of the frontal lobe) and limbic system (including various organs like the amygdala and hippocampus) are primarily responsible for cultivating negative self-talk. The PFC is the thought-producing part, and the limbic system provides the memories and emotions. Can we consciously or subconsciously access our PFC and/or limbic system?

As the central command center of your brain, your frontal lobe links information back and forth across other brain regions and has the vastest neural network and the most reciprocal interconnections with other brain structures . . . The high capacity of your frontal lobe hardware and the rich opportunities to rewire its software through complex thinking set you and all humans far above all other life forms. From early adolescence to young adulthood, the frontal lobes, and the intricate connections between them, are undergoing dramatic functional and structural changes that remodel the brain's complex connectivity and advance its capacity to engage in integrated, reasoned, and high-level thinking . . . You can strengthen the brainpower of your frontal lobe every day of your life.

Here are a few tips to maximize your frontal lobe function:

Avoid automatic pilot: Thoughtful, deep, and effortful processing achieved by your frontal brain regions are key ingredients to building brain health. A brain on automatic pilot is a bored brain. Keep your brain actively curious and challenge yourself to stretch your thinking every day.

Decrease information exposure: Too much information freezes your brain's dynamic frontal lobe capacity to engage in clear thinking and discerning decision-making. You and your brain get overwhelmed by too much information. Your frontal lobes need to be deployed not only to focus on important data, but even more importantly to know what information to ignore. Keep your key frontal lobe operations finely tuned by actively blocking, discarding, and ignoring less relevant tasks and information.

Move beyond memory: ...memory appears to work independently of strategic frontal lobe functions. Your strategic frontal lobes are adept at transforming information to be remembered into bigger, even original, ideas. In fact, trying to remember too many details counteracts the high efficiency of frontal lobe thinking.

Go full frontal: Invest in your cognitive command center for ingenious thinking daily. Doing so will reap bountiful rewards for you both personally and professionally. There is no downside to thinking more strategically by harnessing your frontal lobe potential every day. (Chapman, 2013)

Clearly, we have the power to make real and significant changes to how our PFC and limbic system work together. By harnessing the ability to make improvements to our PFC, we can then move on to regulating how our PFC organizes and creates our thoughts, including negative self-talk. Exercise your brain with puzzles—it's a great way to improve your reasoning and problem-solving skills. The better your PFC works, and the more you consciously work on it, the easier it will be to control your NST.

Since the prefrontal cortex works to connect multiple regions of the brain and combine their functions, you have to get control of your limbic system as well. "The cortex receives input from the outside environment through the sense organs, which in turn shoot messages through at least a part of the limbic system. That's why we feel before we think. However, if we speed up or strengthen the cortex's natural ability to inhibit the limbic system, we can change our feelings before they have a chance to impair our behavior or judgment" (Whitbourne, 2012).

Whitbourne also provides a simple process for getting control of the imbalance of our limbic system:

Examine your irrational beliefs. We often have irrational beliefs that lead us to see threat where no threat actually exists. Most of these beliefs involve our need to live up to life's "must's." Find a more realistic balance between your ideal and your actual self, and your worries will retreat.

Learn how to talk your way through your feelings.
In cognitive-behavioral therapy, clients learn to
counter their illogical thoughts with more clear-headed
analyses. Much of this process involves substituting
the negative ways people think with more neutral or
positive thoughts. Set your feelings aside when you
make important decisions. Many people like to trust
their gut reactions when, in fact, it's precisely those
reactions they should avoid. We are easily swayed by
emotional arguments . . . the more you can separate
logic from emotion, the more likely it is that you'll
make fair and reasoned choices.

Get support from someone who can help you. Our
emotions react quickly and strongly to certain
experiences, and try as we might, we can't rein in those
feelings. This is why sponsors are so crucial to
programs such as Alcoholics Anonymous. That other
person can serve as your "cortex" when your own is
heavily under the influence of an addiction that is
ruling your limbic system.

Build confidence in your self-control. According to
the notion of self-efficacy, people can gain control
over their problematic behaviors when they see
themselves as able to exert that control. As you gain
strength from good decisions, from conquering your
worries, or controlling your impulses, you gradually
find that those impulses and fears dominate you less
and less.

What makes us distinctly human is our ability to use our cortex to override the emotional storms that brew in our subcortical brain regions, like the limbic system. By controlling your worries and emotions, you'll not only make better decisions, but feel better because you have control. (Whitbourne, 2012)

Let's get to work on retraining our brains! Through these simple exercises, you can strengthen your prefrontal cortex, learn to sense your worries and emotions, and find control over your brain.

Prefrontal Cortex Conditioning

First, settle yourself into a comfortable position in a quiet space. Examine your environment, considering ways you can challenge and build your thinking. Is there a puzzle book on the side table you could spend some time working on? Is there a murder mystery movie on that helps you with your critical-thinking skills? What can you find to help you improve your thinking and reasoning?

Evidence shows that a well-developed prefrontal cortex with strong Executive Functions can improve both academic and life outcomes. But very little sweat need be shed while exercising our prefrontal cortex. What it takes is intentional use and practice of the Executive Functions. The fun part is that the workout is most effective when you feel socially supported, happy, relaxed and are physically fit.

1) Put on your rose colored glasses. Create a positive future story; optimism is associated with rising levels of dopamine which engages the brain.

2) Follow a sleep routine. At the end of the day, choose a pleasant activity that brings your day to a peaceful end. Getting adequate sleep is connected with memory function.

3) Deny the drama and avoid getting caught up in gossip, what-if's, and theatrical reactions (other people's too). Drama fires up the amygdala that gets the prefrontal cortex off its game.

4) Move your body with sports, dance, martial arts, yoga, or other active pursuits.

5) Find ways to express your gratitude. Gratitude activities increase positive emotions which then activates the prefrontal cortex.

6) Offer and receive physical contact. Give and take hugs to literally soothe the brain with calming inhibitory peptides.

7) Create silly sentences, acronyms, and cartoons to help remember things. These skills call on the prefrontal cortex and Executive Functions to access working memory. By integrating jokes, riddles, and puns you can also learn to think flexibly by shifting between different meanings and associations of words.

8) Play! Make-believe play in particular strengthens Executive Functions.

9) Be of service and volunteer. The social and mental activity required sends blood rushing to the prefrontal cortex.

10) Learn to juggle. Learning any new and engaging activity fires off neurons in a positive way. Other activities that require focus and practice such as dancing, circus arts, music, and theatre are predicted to significantly strengthen Executive Function. (Dali, 2014)

Work hard to strengthen that executive function and you will find it far easier to control the power, and indeed the creation, of negative self-talk. Let's see if we can find some exercises for the limbic system!

Limbic System Training

"The limbic system gathers information about your current environment, figuring out if there is any kind of immediate threat and then signaling for the immune system, hormones, or nervous system to respond as needed. The limbic system also includes aspects of memory and emotional intelligence. Neuroplasticity allows for retraining the limbic system to optimize function. But there is a theory called the 'limbic loop.' This refers to limbic system dysfunction or the chronic stress response . . . to past traumas" (Shippy, 2020).

When you are caught in the limbic loop, your mind and body are on constant alert—ready to flee or fight at any moment. When you are in that state, it is nearly impossible to control the manifestations of negative self-talk that bloom in this unbalanced environment in your brain.

The best options for limbic system retraining are meditation and neurofeedback. Not everyone can afford the cost of neurofeedback, so let's focus on mindfulness meditation. Finding where you connect your mind to your body, and your body to the earth, is a great way to refocus your stress and relieve yourself of negative energy. Get ready to get Zen!

Mindfulness Meditation

> *Step one*: Understand what's meant by mindfulness: It's about drawing our attention to the present moment in a curious and nonjudgmental way. Mindfulness teaches us to notice our thoughts and feelings when they drift to the past, stumble into the future, or begin to fill us with worry, regret, or numbness that distracts from what is going on right in front of us. Start by focusing on pleasant moments (e.g. that first sip of coffee in the morning, reuniting with a loved one after a long day, that endorphin filled post workout walk or drive home). You'll be ready to manage the harder stuff when life's challenges come your way.

> *Step two*: Breathing is a key mindfulness practice because it is something we always do out of necessity, and it's also a good way to bring our awareness back to the here and now. Taking three or four deep breaths (and paying attention to them) at any given moment can help you calm down and focus.

Step three: Anchor yourself to the physical world. Not feeling your breath? Sit down and notice how the chair you are sitting in feels under your body. Notice the different points of pressure where your butt and lower back touch the chair in different spots. Put your hands flat on the counter or a table, and notice how the hard, cool surface feels. Keep a soft, smooth stone handy and notice its weight as you hold it in your hand and run your fingers across it. These and similar actions will bring your awareness into the present. (Schaeffer, 2018)

That present awareness is part of what pulls the power from negative self-talk. NST resides and thrives in the past. Mindful meditation keeps you focused on the present, moment by moment, and allows your limbic system to rest, de-stress, and refocus. It will take time and effort to fully retrain the brain; you will struggle and stutter and experience false starts. But none of that matters. What matters is that you *never give up*! Another powerful nonconventional method of healing the wounds of negative self-talk is the process of categorizing your memories.

Chapter 14: Categorize Your Memories

Every memory we have we can attach an emotion to: happiness, sadness, desire, frustration, joy, guilt, fear, anxiety, anger, hatred, love, compassion . . . the list is only limited by our ability to feel. So let's create some categories for our memories and organize them in our mind.

1. Happy Memories: What are some of the happiest moments in your life? Be specific and write down no less than 10 memories:

_____

_____

_____

_____

_____

_____

_____

_____

_____

_____

_____

_____

_____

_____

_____

_____

_____

_____

_____

_____

_____

_____

_____

_____

_____

_____

_____

_____

2. Unhappy Memories: Though it could cause you some pain, write down your 10 most painful, unhappy memories.

_____

_____

_____

_____

_____

_____

_____

_____

_____

_____

_____

_____

_____

_____

_____

_____

_____

_____

_____

_____

_____

_____

_____

_____

_____

_____

_____

_____

_____

3. Now, write down at least 10 memories that you have a
   more or less neutral feeling about.

_____

_____

_____

_____

_____

_____

_____

_____

_____

_____

_____

_____

_____

_____

_____

_____

_____

_____

_____

_____

_____

_____

_____

_____

_____

_____

_____

Now we are going to assign each memory to a person who was a part of that experience. For the bad memories, think about the person whose voice you hear in NST when you think of that memory.

Happy Memory
Person Most Associated With It

_____

_____

_____

_____

_____

_____

_____

_____

_____

_____

_____

_____

_____

_____

_____

_____

_____

_____

_____

_____

_____

_____

_____

_____

_____

_____

_____

_____

Bad Memories
Person Most Associated With It

_____

_____

_____

_____

_____

_____

_____
_____
_____
_____
_____
_____
_____
_____
_____
_____
_____
_____
_____
_____
_____
_____
_____
_____
_____
_____

Neutral Memories
Person Most Associated With It

_____
_____
_____
_____

_____

_____

_____

_____

_____

_____

_____

_____

_____

_____

_____

_____

_____

_____

_____

_____

_____

_____

How many different people did you list in the Happy Memories list? What about the Bad Memories list? Who showed up in the Neutral Memories list? Examine each list and analyze why you think each person ended up on each list.

Really think about why each person is connected with that particular memory.

_____

_____

_____

_____

_____

_____

_____

_____

_____

_____

_____

_____

_____

_____

_____

_____

_____

_____

_____

_____

_____

What important connections did you make? Who is most often associated with negative or bad memories? Is it a specific person (parent) or a specific *type* of person (boyfriend/girlfriend)? Which name(s) do you most associate with negative self-talk? Once you know the name(s), you are going to write a brief letter to them telling them that you are done allowing them to control your present from the past. Take back the power!

Chapter 15: Take Back the Power

Negative self-talk is part of our brain processes. For some, it's worse than others. But now that you know how your brain works, how you can optimize your thinking, how you can minimize bad memories, and who it is that is most connected with your bad memories, it's time to set yourself free and take back your power.

> You give away your power any time you allow other people or circumstances to control the way you think, feel, or behave. On the other hand, when you decide that no one will have the power to control how you feel about yourself, how you think about the world, what kind of day you're going to have, how you're going to spend your time, or who you're going to spend it with, you'll empower yourself to create your best life. Empower yourself by thinking before you react. It takes hard work to retain your personal power when you're used to giving it away. But increasing your mental strength requires you to retain every ounce of personal power for yourself. So monitor your personal power, and look for ways in which you are voluntarily giving it away. Retaining your power allows you to devote your time and energy to the things you want, which is key to improving your psychological well-being. (Morin, 2020)

It's time to write a letter to the person or people who've been taking your power for far too long. You can say whatever you want in this letter, but the keys are to take the power away from them, forgive them (if you can), and tell them how great your life is going to be now that they can't steal your power through negative self-talk.

_____

_____

_____

_____

_____

_____

_____

_____

_____

_____

_____

_____

_____

_____

_____

_____

_____

_____

_____

_____

_____

_____

_____

Remember: **YOU** have control of your mind. **YOU** have control of your thoughts. **YOU** have your power back!

Every time you are tempted to react in the same old way, ask yourself if you want to be a prisoner of the past or a pioneer of the future.
—Deepak Chopra

Step 4: Rewire at Will

Ask yourself this question: How am I doing right now? Do I feel empowered and inspired? Do I feel drained and cleansed? Do I feel at least happier than when I started?

This book has given you information, education, elucidation, and advice. Have you reached your goal of being able to rewire your brain? Yes! Good for you! If you are still struggling a bit, go back and start over. Not everyone can get through this the first time, particularly if they suffered from extensive bullying, trauma, or abuse. It will take time and a lot of patience. Be patient with yourself. If you struggle hourly with negative self-talk, just one time through this book and its exercises probably won't be enough. You will need to work on this for a while—hopefully with a therapist and/or support group. Remember: *you don't have to do this alone.*

If you are at this point and have done so alone, and you don't think you've been successful, seek out some support and guidance. It might take you some time to find the right therapist or the right support system, but you need the help.

You can make it, but it's easier if you don't have to do it alone.
—Betty Ford

Chapter 16: Find Your Positive Energy

Early on in this book, we talked about where positive energy comes from. It is in every atom of every molecule of every cell of your body. There is positive energy in the air around us, in the people who love us, and in the nature provided by earth. While mindful meditation is a great way to tap into that positive energy, you can also do it by focusing on certain things.

Without doubt, if you want to succeed in anything you have to develop and attract positive energy into your life to be the successful and dynamic person you want to be. Even if you are naturally shy and introverted, it is not as difficult or as daunting as it first seems. If you want to attract positive energy from the Universe, then you have to be prepared to be the complete package, which is not impossible as long as you are prepared to make a few adjustments to your life. The strategy, a key part of powerful positive thinking, is the action that will help you deliver the person that is already there. It means rejecting irrational fears and anxieties; no longer dwelling in the past, being open minded, tolerant, and slow to anger. Positive energy also demands enthusiasm for life. If you care passionately about something others will lock into that enthusiasm, drive, and commitment and will offer you support and will be prepared to listen to what you have to say. Avoid concentrating on the negatives in your life. By thinking about them you give them energy the universe and the law of attraction will assume that's what you want—so get them out of your head. You have to work at it, accept the odd failures and setbacks, but never forget that the main objective is to turn on that positive energy in your life—the Universe is listening, and it starts now. (Powerful, 2021)

Let's do some exercises to see how well you can tap into that positive energy in the universe!

1. What daily thoughts, actions, or feelings can you give up and replace with positive energy?

_____
_____
_____
_____
_____
_____
_____
_____
_____
_____

2. What people or relationships do you need to cut out of your life because they are toxic?

_____
_____
_____
_____

_____
_____
_____
_____
_____
_____
_____

3. What are you passionate about? What can you do in your day-to-day life to attract positive energy?

_____
_____
_____
_____
_____
_____
_____
_____

4. Define the person you want to be. Do you want to be the person everyone comes to with their problems? Do you want to be the person everyone says always has a smile? Who do you want to be?

_____
_____
_____
_____
_____
_____

_____

_____

_____

_____

5. List some ways you can make subtle changes in your
   life to attract more positive energy:

_____

_____

_____

_____

_____

_____

_____

_____

If you are ready to cut loose bad relationships, redefine who it is you want to be, find your passion and chase it, and spread good cheer, you will attract enormous amounts of positive energy from the universe! Use that positive energy to drown out any negative self-talk that tries ever so desperately to get your attention again.

NST is not going to give up without a fight. You need every tool in this book to help you get your mind strong enough, flexible enough, and positive enough to allow the real you to break through. When people start to notice the difference, you will find them wanting to be around you. They will share their positive energy with you, and you can share yours with them! One way to ensure this victory is to eliminate all your negative energy.

Chapter 17: Eliminate Your Negative Energy

Negative energy exists side by side with positive energy. Which side do you want to be on? We know now that we have to exude positive energy to attract it. You can't get positive energy from the universe or others when you are a grumpy, sad, depressed, anxious mess all the time. Would you want to be around that? So how do we dump the negative energy? There are multiple exercises and techniques you can use to clear out negative energy.

> Negative energy is a toxin to your system. And while you can often endure negativity in your mind and body for prolonged periods (even to the point of it becoming a fundamental trait of your personality), negativity ultimately does you no good. Therefore, becoming and staying free from negative emotions and energy is [an] important strategy. To begin the healing process, you will need to clear negative energy from your system in order to allow positive energy to thrive.

Make Meditation a Regular Part of Your Life
Spending time in the stillness of meditation has a profoundly healing effect on the mind and [in] helping to restore your entire system to balance and positivity. It does this in three crucial ways. First, meditation is the antidote to the stress response that's driven by excessive bad energy. Muscle tension is released, blood pressure and respiration are lowered, stress hormones are minimized, and the fight-or-flight reactivity is

down-regulated through meditation. Second, meditation helps you to witness your thoughts rather than being caught up in an interpretation or evaluation. By witnessing your thoughts as they come and go, you interrupt their stream before a negative interpretation is able to take root in your mental garden. Third, by repeatedly entering into the field of pure consciousness, the negative evaluations in your awareness are washed away, releasing their hold on you.

Get Out into Nature
Nature therapy is a powerful tool to scrub the negative energy from your mind and body. The purity of nature often creates a "system reboot" that helps uninstall negativity from your mental hard drive. When embracing the beauty and majesty of a mountain range, an old growth forest, the ocean, or a midnight star field, it becomes very difficult for negative energy blocks to maintain its hold on your awareness.

Move Your Body
Negative energy loves inertia and lethargy. Like a black hole collapsing in on itself, the negative mindset wants to suck you down into oblivion. One surefire way to break out of the downward spiral is to get up and move your body. Whether by performing some yoga, going for a brisk walk or run, or another form energetic movement, vigorously moving your body helps purge negativity from your system on several levels.

First, it activates your subtle energetic system where negative impressions often get stuck. When the power is flowing without interference, the negativity begins to break up.

Second, with an increase in respiration and circulation, toxins (such as residual stress hormones) get flushed out through deeper breathing and sweat. Third, during energetic physical activity, your body's need for increased oxygen overrides any negative subtext that might try to drag you down; in other words, it's hard to stay focused on the negative when your heart rate and breathing are at a higher pace.

Go Complaint-Free

Complaining is one of the ways negative energy sustains itself in a perpetual motion cycle. When you're focused on negative emotions, you complain about things more, you pay more attention to what irritates you, which makes you feel more negative, and you complain again. It's a never-ending feedback loop of griping and grievances. The simple truth is this: complaining really doesn't solve anything. If you have constructive advice for how something can be improved, great. If not, you're only adding another layer to the surplus of negativity in the world. Chronic complaining is really a symptom of a close relative of negativity: self-pity. It keeps you locked in a perpetual state of "poor me" and not having to take responsibility for your interpretations or how you're feeling. When you commit to going complaint-free for a day or two, or even a week, it has a profound effect on the free-floating negativity you harbor in your consciousness. Negativity feeds on complaints and gripes and when you stop complaining, you begin to starve your negativity of sustenance.

Smile Often
Although you may think of smiling as a simply sentimental or aesthetic activity, there is true magic in your smile. You know that a smile is contagious to others, but because every cell of your body is eavesdropping on every other cell, a smile isn't localized just to your face. Every time you smile, a unique cocktail of neuropeptides are released that help to fight off the effects of stress, lower blood pressure, and act as an overall mood-lifter. Naturally, these effects make it difficult to sustain a negative mood. Consider the face of a chronically negative person. It's not likely they often beam a great smile. Indeed, it's likely the exact opposite; a frown, scowl, or perhaps even a glare, but not a smile. (Brady, 2019)

What amazing words of advice! One of the best things about exploring how to eliminate negative self-talk is that you will learn not only to get rid of it, but also how to make your overall health better! Let's do some quick exercises to work on getting rid of our negative energy.

1. What toxic thoughts do you want to expel from your system right this moment?

_____

_____

_____

_____

_____

_____

_____

_____

_____

_____

_____

2. What negative self-evaluations do you want to see washed away during your practice of meditation?

_____

_____

_____

_____

_____

_____

3. Can you commit to doing meditation on a regular basis? Write down your commitment, whether it be once a week or once a day.

_____

_____

_____

_____

_____

_____

_____

4. When was the last time you were outside and embraced nature? What would you like to do to embrace nature? How often can you do it?

_____
_____
_____
_____
_____
_____
_____
_____
_____
_____

5. When was the last time you moved with purpose? Broke a sweat? Played a sport or did some running? What can you do starting now to include purposeful body movement to your daily routine?

_____
_____
_____
_____
_____
_____
_____
_____
_____
_____

6. How many times a day do you complain? Keep track for one day, write that number here, and then figure out whether they were genuine problems in need of a solution or just you complaining and moaning.

_____

_____

_____

_____

_____

_____

_____

7. How often do you smile each day? What makes you smile, without fail? Is it a kitty or puppy acting silly? Is it your significant other or child(ren)? Is it as simple as the breeze across your face? Think of some things that always make you smile. Then find pictures of these things and post them around your home and workspace. What will you post?

_____

_____

_____

_____

_____

_____

_____

_____

You are on the road to removing excess negative energy from your universe! When your mind and body are aligned in good balance, with a focus on positive instead of negative energy, you will have the ability to tap into the mental and spiritual strength you need to stave off negative self-talk every day!

Chapter 18: Tap into Your Strength—Mental and Spiritual

Having all of your energies in the right place will make it easier for you to tap into the stronger mind and spirit you have inside. You've exercised your prefrontal cortex for exceptional executive function skills, and you've meditated your way to a calmer limbic system.

Now it's time to use those strengths *against* negative self-talk. We're going to present some scenarios here. Write down what your first thought would normally be—whether it's negative self-talk or not. Then write down what you think your first thought should be. How will you alter your thinking process? Be specific in your answers, using the tools we have presented to you. How will you engage your brain? How will you use mindfulness to tap into your spirit?

Scenario 1: It's time for your 20-year high school reunion! Do you plan to go? Why or why not? What is the first thought that comes to mind, and where does that thought lead you? What people or places come into your mind and what energy is attached to them, positive or negative?

_____

_____

_____

_____

_____

_____

_____

_____

Scenario 2: Your company is having a huge holiday party to celebrate the end of a successful year. Nearly everyone you work with is going to be there. What is the first thing you think of? Is it positive or negative? How can you change it to make it better? What skills will you use to tap into your strengths?

_____

_____

_____

_____

_____

_____

_____

_____

_____

_____

Scenario 3: Your partner has asked for your hand in marriage. What is your initial reaction? What skills and tools will you use in this situation? Do you simply react, or do you take it all in and then proactively respond?

_____

_____

_____

_____

_____

_____

_____

_____

_____

Scenario 4: Your boss asks you to stop by the office on your way out today. What is your first thought? What are you feeling right now? Do you need to prepare for the worst, or can you proactively control your thoughts and make adequate preparations for the meeting? How will you handle this?

_____

_____

_____

_____

_____

_____

_____

_____

_____

Scenario 5: You just found out your partner cheated on you. What is the first thought in your mind? What is your first emotion? What *should* your first emotion be? How will you handle this situation? How will you avoid letting this become a source for negative self-talk?

_____

_____

_____

_____

_____

_____

_____

_____

_____

As you probably noticed, these scenarios could happen to anyone. What's critical is that you acknowledge and write down your *very first thought*. Remember, negative self-talk is born from an instant emotional reaction to an external stimulus. You need to determine if that first thought is in fact negative self-talk. If it is, you need to eliminate it and pursue a rational line of thinking. Let go of your fears or triggers and look at each situation objectively. Allow your prefrontal cortex to take in the information, look at it reasonably, and then make a decision about your reaction.

When you are able to do this as a matter of habit, you will have successfully learned how to rewire your brain at will! This can only mean a life filled with more happiness, more control, and more opportunities to be the person you know you are.

Chapter 19: Visualize Your Future without NST

It's time for the final step in the process: visualizing your future without NST. Visualization is a powerful tool, but it's one that must be used only when your mind and body are in homeostasis. Presence of toxic thoughts or toxic people will influence or even stop a positive visualization.

Your brain is constantly using visualization in the process of simulating future experiences, but this process happens so naturally that you generally aren't even aware of it, the same way you usually aren't aware that you are breathing. If you aren't aware of it then you aren't actively directing the process. You can learn to use visualization to actively create future simulations that can help you improve the goals that you set for yourself.

You can create two types of simulations: outcome and process. An outcome simulation is a sensory-based representation of the final outcome you expect, and a process situation involves simulating the steps that get you to the final outcome. Research shows that to get the most benefit from simulations, it is best to use both types together. Also, as you create your simulation using the participant perspective instead of the observer perspective has been shown to be most effective. You don't want to see yourself in the simulation, you want to see it through your eyes as if you are a part of the simulated experience. The more details you have in a visualization the more real it will seem, and the more it will increase performance as the brain starts to develop neural connections that result from the repeated visual image along with enhancing motivation that increases the likelihood of taking an action toward your goal. The more real or true you believe something to be, the more emotional impact it has on you. To really enhance a simulation you want to create as much detail around it as you can so that you begin to feel the experience of it as if it were real. (Vllhauer, 2018)

Visualization is not just about a picture in your head; it is about considering what attainable goals look like. It's about seeing in your mind and feeling in your heart what it is that will make you unbelievably happy. Let's do some visualization exercises to practice.

1. Visualize your dream home. What does it look like? How big is it? What does each room have that you desire? Give us as many details as you can (e.g., colors, smells, and textures).

_____

_____

_____

_____

_____

_____

_____

_____

_____

2. Visualize your perfect job. If you're doing it now, what could make it even better? What do you *really* want your job to be? Do you really want to be your own boss, or do you want a promotion? Visualize what those things look like and write them down.

_____

_____

_____

_____

_____

_____

_____

_____

_____

3. Visualize your dream vacation. Where have you always wanted to go? Where do you find yourself when you think about it? What do you see, smell, hear, and feel? How can you get there?

_____

_____

_____

_____

_____

_____

_____

_____

_____

_____

4. Visualize your perfect family. If you already have a great family, how can you make it better? What aspects of your family dynamic would you want to change? Which ones would you want to keep?

_____

_____

_____

_____

_____

_____

_____

_____

5. Visualize your life without negative self-talk. How wonderful would it be? What things could you do if that voice were gone? How would you feel inside and out without NST? What skills or techniques can you use to get there?

_____

_____

_____

_____

Most of the important things in the world have been accomplished by people who have kept on trying when there seemed to be no hope at all.

—Dale Carnegie

Afterword

It is very difficult to live a life with chronic, unrelenting negative self-talk. The keys to surviving are to always recognize that these thoughts are just chemical transmissions, and that you can't always control them, but you *don't* have to listen to them. Many people who have never tried to cope with or understand their negative self-talk often remain introverted, isolated, and abandoned for the majority of their lives. And it is desperately unfortunate that many of them attempt to or succeed in taking their own lives.

The best thing we, as a community, can do for one another is to be supportive. Being supportive starts with understanding the biology, neurology, and psychology behind negative self-talk. People who struggle with NST don't need you to offer platitudes or empty gestures—they need you to *be there*. They need you to *listen* without interrupting. They need you to *accept* them, negative self-talk and all. Without you, they may feel powerless, hopeless, and alone.

The worst thing we can do, as a community, is write these people off as whackos or nutjobs, turn our backs on them and consider them garbage, or puff out our chests with the pride of our own strength to demonstrate that they are clearly weak and useless.

But here's something you may have never considered: your favorite English professor struggles with NST every day. Your doctor can't stop the NST that invades his mind. The engineer that builds your car or builds our weather satellites can't go through a day without NST telling her she is "nothing." Some of our most successful professionals and contributors to society struggle every single minute of every single day with negative self-talk. They are just good at hiding it.

Once you have completed your transformation and defeated negative self-talk, live your best life! Practice strengthening your brain and your skills. Practice being proactive rather than reactive. Get happy and share your positive energy with the world. Once you reach that point, you have a responsibility to others who struggle with NST. They need your support. They need to see that nothing is hopeless. They need to see that *success is possible.*

So make a commitment today. Commit to always being supportive. Commit to always being an open-minded and active listener. Commit to being a friend to someone who is self-isolating. Commit to finding your understanding of how negative self-talk works. Commit to helping heal the community of negative self-talk.

References

Adult Health. (2021). Forgiveness: Letting go of grudges and bitterness. *Mayoclinic.org.*

Mayo Clinic, Retrieved 24 April 2021 from https://www.mayoclinic.org/healthy- lifestyle/adult-health/in-depth/forgiveness/art-20047692

American Addiction Centers. (2020). The Long Term Effects of Bullying. *Mentalhelp.net.* Retrieved 24 April 2021 from https://www.mentalhelp.net/abuse/long-term-effects-of- bullying/

APA Div. 12. (2017). What Is Cognitive Behavioral Therapy? *apa.org.* Retrieved 13 Mar. 2021 from https://www.apa.org/ptsd-guideline/patients-and-families/cognitive-behavioral

Baker, J. (1991). Will CR Work for Me? *CelebrateRecovery.org.* Retrieved 13 Mar. 2021 from https://www.celebraterecovery.com/will-cr-work

Bargh, J. A., & Morsella, E. (2008). The Unconscious Mind. *Perspectives on Psychological Science : A Journal of the Association for Psychological Science, 3*(1), 73–79. https://doi.org/10.1111/j.1745-6916.2008.00064.x

Bobby, A. (2020). The Twelve Principles of Meditation. *Bodymindlight.com.* Retrieved 24 April 2021 from https://bodymindlight.com/the-twelve-principles-of-meditation

Borton, J., Markowitz, L., & Dieterich, J. (2005). Effects of Suppressing Negative Self–Referent Thoughts on

Mood and Self–Esteem. *Journal of Social and Clinical Psychology, 24*(2). doi.org/10.1521/jscp.24.2.172.62269

Brady, A. (2019). 6 Pathways to Remove Negative Energy from Your Mind and Body. *Chopra.com.* Retrieved 7 May 2021 from https://chopra.com/articles/6-pathways-to- remove-negative-energy-from-your-mind-and-body

Brandt, A. (2017). 4 Ways Childhood Trauma Can Affect Adults: When we bury our feelings, we bury who we are. *Psychologytoday.com.* Retrieved 6 May 2021 from https://www.psychologytoday.com/us/blog/mindful -anger/201706/4-ways-childhood-trauma-can-affect-adults

Brem, A. K., Ran, K., & Pascual-Leone, A. (2013). Learning and memory. *Handbook of Clinical Neurology, 116,* 693–737. https://doi.org/10.1016/B978-0-444-53497-2.00055-3

Bressert, S. (2016). What to Expect in Your First Counseling Session. *Psychcentral.com.* Retrieved 24 April 2021 from https://psychcentral.com/lib/what-to-expect-in-your-first- counseling-session#1

Brownstein, J. (2009). Swayze: Outlived Most With Pancreatic Cancer - Fighting for 20 months, Swayze outlived most with his diagnosis. *Abcnews.go.com.* Retrieved 13 Mar. 2021 from https://abcnews.go.com/Health/PatrickSwayze/patr ick-swayzes-death-shows-tough-pancreaticcancer/story?id=8583819

Buck, N. (2013). Mental Health and Happiness. *PsychologyToday.com.* Retrieved 29 April 2021 from https://www.psychologytoday.com/us/blog/peacefu l-parenting/201308/mental- health-and-happiness-2

Chapman, S. (2013). Go Full Frontal to Be Smart: How harnessing the power of your frontal lobes maximizes your brain's potential. *PsychologyToday.com*. Retrieved 6 May 2021 from https://www.psychologytoday.com/us/blog/make-your-brain-smarter/201301/go- full-frontal-be-smart

Chosdosh, S. (24 Aug. 2016). Mind Aglow: Scientists Watch Thoughts Form in the Brain. *Scientific American*, Retrieved https://www.scientificamerican.com/article/mind-aglow- scientists-watch-thoughts-form-in-the-brain/

Cramer, S., Sur, M., Dobkin, B., et al. (June 2011). Harnessing neuroplasticity for clinical Applications. *Brain 134* (6), 1591–1609. https://doi.org/10.1093/brain/awr039

Dali Lama Center for Peace and Education. (2014). 10 Exercises for Your Prefrontal Cortex. *Heartmindonline.org*. Retrieved 6 May 2021 from https://heartmindonline.org /resources/10-exercises-for-your-prefrontal-cortex

Exploring Your Mind. (2020). Freud on Developing a Strong Sense of Self. *Exploringyourmind.com*. Retrieved 25 April 2021 from https://exploringyourmind .com/freud-developing-a-strong-sense-of-self/

Flannery, B. (2021). A List of Coping Skills for Anger, Anxiety, and Depression. *Infinite Mindcare*. Retrieved 7 Apr. 2021 from https://www.infinitemindcare.com/single-post/2016/12/18/a-list-of-coping-skills-for-anger-anxiety-and-depression

Flaxington, B. (2020). The Destructive Nature of Negative Self-Talk: Turn your attention toward the positive. *Psychology Today*. Retrieved 7 Apr. 2021 from https://www.psychology today.com/us/blog/understand-other-people/202002/the-destructive-nature-negative-self-talk

Fox, K., Dixon, M., Nijeboera, S., Girna, M., Floman, J., Lifshitz, M., Ellamild, M., Sedlmeiere, P., and Christoff, K. (2016). Functional neuroanatomy of meditation: A review and Meta-analysis of 78 functional neuroimaging investigations. *Neuroscience and Biobehavioral Reviews, 605*, 208-228.

Genomind. (2019). Conquer the Bully in your Brain. *Genomind.com*, Retrieved 23 Mar. 2021 from https://www.genomind.com/blog/ways-stop-negative-self-talk

Gordon, S. (2020). The Long-Lasting Effects of Bullying. *Verywellfamily.org*. Retrieved 6 May 2021 from https://www.verywellfamily.com/bullying-impact-4157338

Hartney, E. (2020). How Emotional Pain Affects Your Body. *Verywellmind.org*. Retrieved 4 May 2021 from https://www.verywellmind.com/physical-pain-and-emotional-pain-22421

Health Direct. (nd). Bullying. Australian Government Dept. of Health. *Healthdirect.gov.au*. Retrieved 24 April 2021 from https://www.healthdirect.gov.au/bullying

Health Encyclopedia. (2021). Journal for Mental Health. *University of Rochester Medical Center.* Retrieved 23 April 2021 from https://www.urmc.rochester.edu/encyclopedia /content.aspx?contentid=4552&contenttypeid=1#:~ :text=Journaling%20helps%20control%20your%20sy mptoms,and%20identifying%20negative%20thoughts %20and James, A. (2021).

Understanding Emotional Agony and How It Changes Us. *Betterhelp.com.* Retrieved 4 May 2021 from https://www.betterhelp.com/advice/grief/understan ding- emotional-agony-and-how-it-changes-us/

Johnson, S. B., Blum, R. W., & Giedd, J. N. (2009). Adolescent maturity and the brain: the promise and pitfalls of neuroscience research in adolescent health policy. *The Journal of adolescent health : official publication of the Society for Adolescent Medicine, 45*(3), 216–221. https://doi.org/10.1016/j.jadohealth.2009.05.016

Kranz, B. (2017). What is Biofeedback? *Healthline.com.* Retrieved 16 Mar. 2021 from https://www.healthline.com/health/biofeedback

Lechner, T. (2019). Chakra Cleansing: How to Clear Your Chakras & Free Your Energy. *Chopra.com.* Retrieved 25 April 2021 from https://chopra.com/articles/chakra-cleansing-how-to-clear-your-chakras-and-free-your-energy

Legg, T.J. (2019). Managing Suicidal Ideation. *Healthline.com*, Retrieved https://www.healthline.com/health/suicidal-ideation

Martin, B. (2016). Challenge Negative Self-Talk. *Psych Central.* Retrieved 22 Mar. 2021 from https://psychcentral.com/lib/challenging-negative-selftalk#1

Mayo Clinic Staff. (2020). 7 tips to live a happier life. *Mayoclinic.com*. Retrieved 29 April 2021 from https://www.mayoclinichealthsystem.org/hometown-health/speaking-of- health/7-tips-to-live-a-happier-life

Mayo Clinic Staff. (2021). Support Groups: Make Connections, Get Help. *Mayoclinic.com*. The Mayo Clinic. Retrieved 24 April 2021 from https://www.mayoclinic.org/healthy- lifestyle/stress-management/in-depth/support-groups/art-20044655

McGraw, Phillip C. (Executive Producer). (2002-present). *The Dr. Phil Show* [TV Series]. Petesky Productions; CBS.

Morin, A. (2016). 9 Ways for You to Keep Your Personal Power. *Psychologytoday.com*. Retrieved 25 April 2021 from https://www.psychologytoday.com/us/blog/what-mentally-strong-people-dont-do/201601/9-ways-you-keep-your-personal-power

Morin, A. (2020). 2 Exercises That Will Help You Take Back Your Power: You give away your power any time you allow other people to control you. *PsychologyToday.com*. Retrieved 7 May 2021 from https://www.psychologytoday.com/us/blog/what-mentally- strong-people-dont-do/202002/2-exercises-will-help-you-take-back-your-power

National Institute of Neurological Disorders and Stroke. (2019). Brain Basics: Understanding Sleep. *Nih.gov*, Retrieved https://www.ninds.nih.gov/Disorders/Patient-Caregiver- Education/Understanding-Sleep

Neuroagility. (2021). About qEEG and Neurofeedback. *Neuroagility.com*, Retrieved 23 Mar. 2021 from https://neuroagility.com/neurofeedback/

Norris, D. (2018). Some thoughts on thoughts: The inner critic and self-talk. *Ct.Counseling.org*. Retrieved 23 April 2021 from https://ct.counseling.org/2018/12/some-thoughts-on- thoughts-the-inner-critic-and-self-talk/

Powerful Positive Thinking. (2021). How to attract Positive energy from the Universe. *Powerfulpositivethinking.org*. Retrieved 7 May 2021 from https://www.powerfulpositivethinking.org/how-to-attract-positive-energy-from-the-universe/

Psychology Today. (2021). Catastrophizing. *PsychologyToday.com*, Retrieved 23 Mar. 2021 from https://www.psychologytoday.com/us/basics/catastrophizing

Psychology Today. (2021). Self-Talk. *Psychologytoday.com*. Retrieved 10 Mar. 2021 from https://www.psychologytoday.com/us/basics/self-talk

Purves, D., Augustine, GJ., Fitzpatrick, D., et al., editors. (2001). *Neuroscience*. 2nd edition. Sinauer Associates. Excitatory and Inhibitory Postsynaptic Potentials. Available from: https://www.ncbi.nlm.nih.gov/books/NBK11117/

Ramesh, M. G., Sathian, B., Sinu, E., & Kiranmai, S. R. (2013). Efficacy of rajayoga meditation on positive thinking: an index for self-satisfaction and happiness in life. *Journal of clinical and diagnostic research : JCDR,* *7*(10), 2265–2267.https://doi.org/ 10.7860/JCDR/2013/5889.3488

Recovery Dharma. (2020). What is Recovery Dharma? *RecoveryDharma.org.* Retrieved 13 Mar. 2021 from https://recoverydharma.org/what-is-recovery-dharma

Reuell, P. (5 Oct. 2015). How the Brain Builds New Thoughts. *Harvard Gazette,* Retrieved https://news.harvard.edu/gazette/story/2015/10/how-the-brain-builds-new-thoughts/

Rosenberg, G. (2019). What Makes It So Hard to Ask for Help? *Psychologytoday.com.* Retrieved 6 May 2021 from https://www.psychologytoday.com/us/blog/emotional- mastery/201904/what-makes-it-so-hard-ask-help

Schaeffer, C. (2018). 4 Simple Steps to Mindfulness: Here are a few easy ways to increase your attention and calm. *PsychologyToday.com.* Retrieved 6 May 2021 from https:// www.psychologytoday.com/us/blog/psychlopedia/201803/4-simple-steps-mindfulness

Scott, E. (2020). The Toxic Effects of Negative Self-Talk. *Verywellmind.org.* Retrieved 4 May 2021 from https://www.verywellmind.com/negative-self-talk-and-how-it-affects-us-4161304#:~:text=Focusing%20on%20negative%20thoughts%20may,tend%20to%20be%20more%20stressed.

Sehgal, K & Chopra, D. (2019). The surprising benefits of journaling for 15 minutes a day—and 7 prompts to get you started. *CNBC.com.* Retrieved 23 April 2021

from https://www. cnbc. com
/2019/07/25/deepak-chopra-benefits-of-journaling-
and-8-prompts-to-get-you-started.html

Seltzer, L. (2011). The Past: Don't Dwell on It, Revision It!
Part 1- You "loiter" in the past at your own peril.
Psychology Today. Retrieved 22 Mar. 2021 from
https://www. psychology
today.com/us/blog/evolution-the-self/201108/the-
past-dont-dwell-it-revision-it-part-1

Shaffer, J. (2016). Neuroplasticity and Clinical Practice:
Building Brain Power for Health. *Frontiers in psychology,*
7, 1118. https://doi.org/10.3389/fpsyg.2016.01118

Shippy, A. (2020). The Limbic Loop – The Missing Piece Of
Your Healing Puzzle? *Annshippymd.com.* Retrieved 6
May 2021 from https://annshippymd.com/know-
the- root-cause/the-limbic-loop-the-missing-piece-of-
your-healing-puzzle/

Simone, F. (2017). Negative Self-Talk: Don't Let It
Overwhelm You - There are ways to overcome
negative thinking. *Psychology Today.* Retrieved 22 Mar.
2021 from
https://www.psychologytoday.com/us/blog/family-
affair/201712/negative-self-talk-dont- let-it-
overwhelm-you

SMART Recovery. (2021). SMART Recovery for Individuals
with Addictions: Discover "The Power of Choice" in
Recovery. *SmartRecovery.org.* Retrieved 13 Mar. 2021
from
https://www.smartrecovery.org/individuals/?_ga=2.
96556383.1151415920.1615688421-
1790113751.1615688421

Sparks, D. (2019). Mayo Mindfulness: Overcoming negative self-talk. *Mayoclinic.org*. Retrieved 7 Apr. 2021 from https://newsnetwork.mayoclinic.org/discussion/mayo-mindfulness- overcoming-negative-self-talk/

Stelter, G. (2016). A Beginner's Guide to the 7 Chakras and Their Meanings. *Healthline.com*. Retrieved 25 April 2021 from https://www.healthline.com/health/fitness-exercise/7-chakras

Sword, K., and Zimbardo, P. (2014). This Is Your Brain: How is this incredibly multi-faceted organ, the brain, affected by trauma? *Psychologytoday.com*, Retrieved 10 Mar. 2021 from https://www. psychologytoday.com/us/blog/the-time-cure/201404/is-your-brain

Szabados, B. (December 1982). Freud, Self-Knowledge and Psychoanalysis. *Canadian Journal of Philosophy, 12*(4), 691-707.

Villines, Z. (2019). 6 Ways the Limbic System Impacts Physical, Emotional, and Mental Health.

GoodTherapy.org. Retrieved 6 May 2021 from https://www.goodtherapy.org/blog/6- ways-the-limbic-system-impacts-physical-emotional-and-mental-health-0316197

Vllhauer, J. (2018). 3 Effective Visualization Techniques to Change Your Life: Proper visual imagery techniques can improve how you feel and how you perform.

Psychologytoday.com. Retrieved 7 May 2021 from https://www.psychologytoday.com /us/blog/living-forward/201806/3-effective-visualization-techniques-change-your-life

Walton, A. (2014). 11 Intriguing Reasons to Give Talk Therapy A Try. *Forbes.com*. Retrieved 29 April 2021 from https://www.forbes.com/sites/alicegwalton/2014/06/03/11-intriguing- reasons-to-give-talk-therapy-a-try/?sh=26523eb64ebb

Whitbourne, S. (2012). Turn Down Your Brain's Worry Center: Control worrying by controlling your brain's worry patterns. *PsychologyToday.com*. Retrieved 6 May 2021 from https://www.psychologytoday.com/us/blog/fulfillment-any-age/201210/turn-down-your- brain-s-worry-center

Work Health Life. (2021). Baby Boomers and Mental Health. *Workhealthlife.com*, Retrieved 23 Mar. 2021 from https://www.workhealthlife.com/Article/PrintDirect/07ca7901-d03b-402d-8579-c4b45fa718b9

Printed in the USA
CPSIA information can be obtained
at www.ICGtesting.com
CBHW071742300724
12433CB00016B/778